Ritual Facilitation:

Collected Articles

on the

Art of Leading Rituals

Shauna Aura Knight

The scanning, uploading and distribution of this book via the Internet or via any other means without the permission of the publisher is illegal and punishable by law. Please purchase only authorized editions and do not participate in or encourage the electronic piracy of copyrighted materials. Your support of the author's rights is appreciated.

This is a work of nonfiction. Names used within this work are either used with the permission of the individual, or are names used to protect the identity of those who chose not to reveal their names. No warranty is implied or given about the use of the information in this book. This book is not intended to treat or diagnose any medical condition.

Ritual Facilitation: Collected Articles on the Art of Leading Rituals

Copyright © Shauna Aura Knight, 2014
Cover Art ® 2014 by Shauna Aura Knight

Electronic Publication Date: April 2014

This book may not be reproduced or used in whole or in part by any means existing without written permission from Shauna Aura Knight.

For more information to learn to more about this, or any other author's work, please **visit**
http://www.ShaunaAuraKnight.com or
http://shaunaaura.wordpress.com

Table of Contents

Dedication 5

Acknowledgments 6

Introduction 7

Section One: Core Skills in Ritual Facilitation 9

Art of Ritual: Tools and Skills for Effective Rituals 10

Raising the Sacred Fire: How to Build and Move Energy in Ritual 18

Reasons to Raise Energy 28

Ritual Design & Facilitation: Ritual Bling and Magical Mood-Setting ... 34

Ritual Design & Facilitation: Managing Complicated Logistics 43

Ritual Design & Facilitation: Accessibility, Learning Modalities, and Logistics 52

Ritual Design & Facilitation: Chanting that Works 61

Additional Chanting Resources 68

Section Two: Ritual Excellence 73

Ritual Design & Facilitation: The Shaman as Ritualist 74

Raising the Bar: Rituals That Pagans Look Forward To 83

Ecstatic Ritual for Communities: Celebratory or Transformative? 89

Section Three: Elusive Authenticity 94

Urban Ecstatic Ritual 95

Authenticity in Ritual 103

Authenticity in Ritual: Going Deeper 111

Deepening Relationship with Deity Through Artwork 119

Section Four: Using Myth and Story to Craft Rituals 124

In the Forge Fires: Transformative Ritual 125

Equinox: Planting Seeds of Rebirth 133

Desire: Reaching for the Rose 143

The Longest Night: Taking Up the Sword... 153

The Longest Night: An Arthurian Ritual and Vigil................................ 161

Art, Ritual, Performance, and Transformation 170

Section Four: Advanced Skills in Ritual..................................178

Ritual Design & Facilitation: Coping with Ritual Disasters 179

Ritual Design & Facilitation: Planning Festival Rituals 188

Ritual: Physical Accessibility, Transgender Inclusion, and more 195

Confidence in Facilitation: Using the Magical Feather 204

Section Four: Safety, Ethics, and Healing in Rituals................213

Safety and Ethics in Rituals and Groups.. 214

Thoughts on Ritual, Psychology, and Therapy 223

Healing From our Past..230

Previously published works in order of appearance: 233

About Shauna Aura Knight 236

Non-Fiction Books by Shauna Aura Knight..238

Anthologies in which Shauna's Work Appears 240

Fiction Books by Shauna Aura Knight 241

Dedication

This book, and my book Awakening the Leader Within, exist because of the love and support of my mom Stephanie. She raised me to believe that there's nothing that I can't do if I try hard enough. Whenever bullies put me down, what my mom instilled in me held me up. "Don't ever let anyone tell you that you can't do that."

I Love you, Mom.

Acknowledgments

This book (and my book Awakening the Leader Within) would simply not be possible without the education I received at the Diana's Grove Mystery School. The skills and tools I learned inspired me to take this work out into the world. It's often difficult to properly cite where some of these tools come from as most of the work at Diana's Grove was taught through team-taught presentations and experiential work, and pulls from many fields of expertise. Whenever I track down a tool or a resource I work to list it.

Diana's Grove no longer exists, but there are others like me working to take that work forward such as work The Grove (www.enterthegrove.com) has been doing in St. Louis.

My work in ecstatic ritual also has a foundation in the Reclaiming tradition, and I'm grateful for the work done by the many members of the Reclaiming tradition in exploring these techniques.

I also learned a number of exceptional skills to add to my ritualist tool belt by taking a series of Shamanic classes with Joan Forest Mage of the Life Force Arts Center.

I want to thank my friend and occasional co-teacher Steve Smith for permission to publish our two co-written articles.

A big thank you to Anne Key and Candace Kant at Goddess Ink press for permission to reprint two of my articles published in their "Stepping Into Ourselves" anthology. And thanks to *CIRCLE Magazine* for the opportunity to publish my articles on ritual facilitation. Many of the articles in this book have been published, or will shortly be published, in *CIRCLE Magazine*.

Introduction

Ritual is a crucial component of spiritual work. And when we work with group rituals, particularly with larger sizes of groups, ritual becomes more complicated. Most people never learned public speaking skills; they learned the mysteries of their own tradition.

Or maybe you said, "Hey, let's work our way through _____ book. We can meet in my living room." And suddenly, *you're leading the rituals.* There are a lot of inherent problems that come up when people facilitate a ritual that have nothing to do with magic, religion, or spirituality and have everything to do with facilitation. These are typically pretty honest mistakes. I honor each and every person out there who has stepped up to facilitate a ritual, particularly those of you who were nervous and nauseated and pretty sure you were going to screw it up by puking on your shoes. (I bet you didn't.)

There are ways to make our rituals better. Sometimes, it means learning a lot of skills that you maybe didn't really want to learn—but you want to better serve your group. So you learn how to project your voice, how to hold your body. Sometimes, it means learning about logistics and that Cakes and Ale works great in a group of 20 but might not work well for 200.

My intention with these articles isn't to teach tradition or theology. It's not to say, "Your tradition is wrong." It's to talk about facilitation techniques, and the impact of certain techniques on the people who are participating in your rituals.

When I talk to Pagans around the country, one of the most common reasons I hear that people don't involve themselves in Pagan groups or events can be summed up as "Bad ritual." We are a growing, learning group of diverse traditions in the Pagan community, and I think we're finally at the point where we can really begin to look at what works, and what doesn't work. Not from the perspective of "My tradition is better than yours," but, "Singing will work to engage people," or, "Standing in line is boring."

I hope that this collection of articles—will help you to design and facilitate stronger, more potent rituals that help you serve the groups you stepped up to serve.

And, hopefully, keep everyone's shoes clean.

"You must do the things you think you cannot do."

—Eleanor Roosevelt

Section One: Core Skills in Ritual Facilitation

Art of Ritual: Tools and Skills for Effective Rituals

First published in the Heartland Spirit January & February 2010

What makes a great ritual? And what makes a ritual boring or unpleasant? Think of the rituals you've attended or facilitated. Which ones called to your soul, and which were terrible. Across traditions, there are facilitation skills that can help you lead more potent rituals. There are also common challenges snags that can take make an ordinary ritual tedious or worse.

Intention
Begin with the context and intention; what's the point? Whether you're planning a ritual from the ground up or using an established liturgy, what is the goal? Celebrating the season, spellwork, personal transformation, building community, honoring a rite of passage? Understanding what goal your ritual should accomplish will help you chose an effective form and appropriate logistics to serve your group.

Audience

Who will celebrate this ritual? Private group, public ritual, or large festival? The number of participants, and if they're part of a community or are at their first ritual, will have an impact.

If you've been to a ritual where 100 people are being smudged one at a time, you might have found yourself getting bored. When the third or fourth go around the circle in the ritual, you may begin to wish you were anywhere else. One-at-a-time logistics can be useful, but they don't always scale to a larger group, and a boring chunk of a ritual can disengage everyone. Look at the intention of what that piece of ritual should accomplish.

If you want each person to purify themselves, choose a token from an altar, have a one-on-one experience with a drawn-down deity, or drink from a communal cup, some options could be having four smudge sticks going around the circle, instead of just one or several people aspecting a deity or element, or having people interact with an element or altar in groups of five. Or perhaps everyone could participate at once with a sound purification by toning.

Location

Will the ritual be indoors at a private home, outdoors in a park, or at a rented venue? This will impact if you can use sage, candles, or a fire. I've attended rituals in large spaces or outdoors where the facilitators were talking on and on, but we couldn't hear them. At a ritual in the park, the ritualists were trying to shout over neighboring parties.

Check out the space for your ritual. If you're burning incense, it's helpful to know about the air flow; I've had to crack open a door at a ritual with a heavy, cloying incense. If you rent a space without a door that shuts, will participants feel safe enough to relax?

Gracing and Welcoming

For a public ritual, you likely have attendees who are shy or nervous. At a recent ritual I had 15 people attending their first ritual. A way to put people at ease and set up your ritual for success is to have greeters. Welcome people warmly, let them know how they can meet their needs for food, drink, the restroom. Give people context for the ritual so they know what's appropriate to do.

Common skills

Many people list public speaking among their greatest fears, but good speaking skills will serve any ritualist.

Volume – A common difficulty is people who offer beautiful poetic liturgies, and I can't hear them. In a larger circle, or for outdoor rituals, you'll need to project a clear, strong voice. Practice with a partner by speaking and increasing the distance between you.

Tone – I can get a lot of volume in my voice, but if I'm screaming, "Can you take a breath together and relax," it probably won't have the intended effect.

Words – For scripted rituals, memorizing your liturgy adds more power to your ritual. When ritualists are fumbling with scripts or forgetting lines, that dissipates the energy. I work in an extemporaneous ritual tradition, so I've practiced how to speak on the fly. When I began taking ritual roles, I was petrified that I'd forget what I was supposed to say.

Then I did forget my words—I was mortified. My mentors were supportive, and I discovered that the earth didn't swallow me up and the ritual continued. My worst fear having happened, I grew more comfortable speaking spontaneously, which helps when surprises arise.

Body Language – If your shoulders are hunched while you lead a meditation inviting people to relax, or standing stiffly while invoking the power of the fire, people may believe what your body is saying, not your words. Practice letting your body communicate just as much as your voice.

Engagement – This is the difference between knowing the performance skills to make your voice sound impassioned, and being impassioned. What can make a ritual really pop is deeply, genuinely connecting to what you're saying. Imagine invoking Isis. Connect to Her, to a woman grieving the loss of her love, the sorrow welling up to flood the Nile. You may not be a deity, but you've probably felt grief.

Connecting to the emotions of the story can bring a more potent experience to your participants. Your engagement draws in others. I have a hard time sinking into a ritual with invocations in a monotone, or even in strident, ringing tone. However, when someone deeply believes or feels the invocation, the charisma of that brings me into the magic of the experience.

Energy Flow

Rituals have an arc; just like a novel or movie, each piece of the plot builds on the next. What does each piece of the ritual need to accomplish to set up the next piece for success? Beginning a ritual with something boring can lay set a pattern for the ritual. However, if you want people to participate in the ritual, setting the tone for that from the beginning will help. If your goal is to get a hundred people chanting and singing and dancing, then each piece of the ritual must build up to that.

If you are taking people down into the Underworld and you hope they will trust the group enough to share an old wound or fear they wish to release there, then your whole ritual must build up the trust for them to do so. Transitions are important too. If between every piece of the ritual someone says, "And now we're going to invoke Air, and now we're going to raise energy," that takes people out of the story and the magic.

Participation

When people participate, they are engaging with the ritual at a deeper level. When we each engage in the chant, light a candle, or speak a word, we're adding our energy. Offering different experiential modalities can help participants connect to the ritual, such as auditory, visual, and kinesthetic. There are many variations, including internal and external processing. Do you learn better through journaling, or talking something out? Offering different ways to participate can keep more people invested. A ritual where one or two people are talking a lot can lose the attention of the kinesthetic and visual folks.

Handling Disruptions

The more people attending the ritual, and the more logistics, the more things that could go wrong. Being able to handle disruptions and changes in the plan with grace is a combination of public speaking skills and learning to speak on the fly. It's also discerning the best way to handle a surprise.

In a recent ritual, a child in attendance rushed into the circle while we told the story of Isis. Instead of rushing in to get the child out of the circle, or pretending like she wasn't there, I worked her into the ritual, "And Isis was joyful to find the energy of the Sun."

Surprises can include barking dogs, cell phones, candles being knocked over. In a ritual where someone's cell phone went off, I said, "There is the sound on the wind, the sound that calls to us as we call to the divine." When dogs are barking loudly, "They feel the wildness of the land. Can you feel it? Will you howl with the hounds to honor the Earth?"

Try to acknowledge the distraction and try to include it. If it's a loud disruption, you might acknowledge it and perhaps wait for things to quiet. Talking over or ignoring interruptions usually results in everyone thinking about the disruption instead of paying attention. If you name the distraction, you can shape where the ritual goes from there even if it wasn't your original plan.

Disruptions can't always be worked in smoothly. While offering a ritual in Iowa City, we were in a park building with uncovered windows. It was dark, and we'd lit a small alcohol fire in a cauldron. As someone began invoking Hestia, I saw outside the park's maintenance vehicle outside.

I figured that from outside, the firelight would look like the building was on fire. I said "Let us invoke Hestia first with the flame unlit," and extinguished the fire to be re-lit later. If I'd said, "Hold on! Let me put out the fire, the park maintenance guy is here!" that would have been more energetically disruptive. Using mythic language, I kept people in a ritual mindset. Because of the fact that the group trusted me as the facilitator, this worked.

Mythic Impact

What happens in ritual can seem bigger; actions and words can take on a mythic. A candle-lighting ceremony can be beautiful and inspiring until the wind picks up and blows out people's light of hope, it can be personally devastating for the people whose candles blow out. You might say, "The winds of change are blowing! Sometimes we must light the light again."

If it rains, you may scrap a logistic completely and say, "Let us sing, light the Light of Hope with our voices, and later in the tent we will light our candles," or something else. What you do in ritual space can have a bigger impact on participants. If you are aware of your impact, and of ritual logistics, you can keep someone from having a negative experience from a logistical snafu.

Feedback

After practice sessions or a public ritual, getting feedback on your work is critical to growth. People may say, "That was the best ritual ever," or, "The energy at this ritual was really bad, it never heated up." Neither is effective feedback.

Good feedback is precise, giving a ritualist tools to improve their work. Specific, I-referenced feedback, "I had a hard time connecting to the energy," is a beginning. More specific is better. "During your Ancestors invocation, your body language was stiff and didn't support what you were asking us to do," or "Your grounding was long for me; it was hard to stand for a long time."

I balance compassion and generosity with feedback; I don't give feedback when someone's had a horrible day, but if I tell someone their Air invocation was perfect when I actually couldn't hear them, I'm not doing them a service.

Feedback Session

After most rituals (or any event) I recommend feedback sessions. Debriefing afterward gives the group a chance to discuss what went well, what didn't go so well, and how to do it better. Having an agreement for feedback can be one of the best things you can do to improve your ritual skills.

Practice

The pressure of a public can be intimidating. Gathering in a safe space to practice can be a great way to try out new ritual skills without the anxiety of many people watching. Practicing elemental invocations, guided meditations, and other pieces of ritual will help you get used to doing them. "Ritual gymnastics" sessions are effective for practicing ritual tools until you feel comfortable.

Building Skill

Many of these are skills built over time. Observe the rituals you attend, and learn to discern what rituals inspire you, which repulse you. You'll gain the information to create stronger, more impactful rituals.

Raising the Sacred Fire: How to Build and Move Energy in Ritual

Published in CIRCLE Magazine Issue 105, Also published in Stepping Into Ourselves: An Anthology of Writing About Priestesses, Goddess Ink Press

Have you ever worked to build ecstatic energy in rituals?

Together we are singing, moving, dancing, chanting, and drumming around the fire in the center of the circle. The energy builds and slows then rises up again. I move the drum beat, and the drum beat moves me. We draw closer; I look into the firelit eyes of people around me and we smile as we sing. We drop the chant down to a whisper, then bring it back up again.

Our song is a prayer for transformation, a prayer for our individual gifts to be transformed on Brigid's Forge into their highest potential. I am singing for my gift, and for the gifts of everyone there. Our prayer is singing, movement, rhythm, and our shared intention. The chant moves into a tone that rises and falls like a fire at the bellows until we hold the silence together.

Raising energy in ritual can be a difficult function to facilitate. Many ritualists get a chant going only to find the group stops singing it as soon as that ritualist pauses to take a breath. Despite the challenges, there are some skills, tools, and processes that you can use to help build potent, transformative energy in rituals.

Facilitating ecstatic energy is the ability to sense energy and the ability to understand the logical energetic flow of any event. Having talent as a singer, drummer, musician, or dancer can help; it's perhaps more important to have a team of people that is engaged, excited, and willing to model the energy as an example. Excitement is contagious, and if you are invested in the energy, then your participants will be more willing to buy into it and commit their energy as well.

What is Energy?

While some ritualists may be gifted with the ability to see auras and energy, I'm not among them. I sense energy more kinesthetically, and I also work with energy less as a metaphysical thing, and more as the life-force cycled from our bodies. Breathing in oxygen, there's a chemical reaction and we exhale carbon dioxide; chemical reactions release energy.

I can also see energy through the physical reality of body language. So sensing energy is largely becoming observant.

Think about the last meeting or class you were at. How were people sitting? Did people look interested or bored and tired? How about the teacher or facilitator, did their voice drone on, or were they excited?

Now think about a concert or sports event. How did you know if people were excited? Were people standing up and cheering or dancing? When people applauded, what did you feel inside?

Notice the environment around you and how you can sense the energy level of the group. Energy comes across in our body language, movements, actions, how we are talking, and the look in our eyes.

If I'm talking to someone and they're not looking at me, I don't feel like they're really interested in me. But if I go to a friend with a problem and they're looking deeply into my eyes, I feel like they are really present and connected to me.

Ways to Add Energy
Here are some ways to add my energy in ritual, broken down by element.

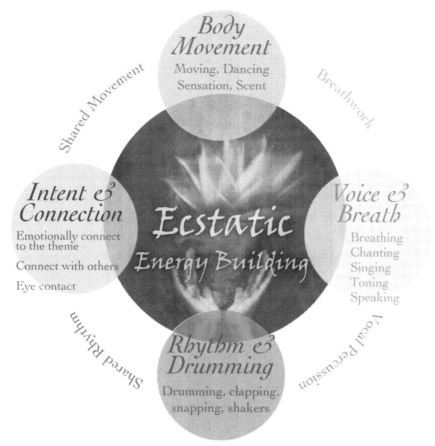

Earth—Body, movement, dancing. Whether I'm a great dancer, or just adding my energy by swaying back and forth to the rhythm of the chant, I'm adding the energy of my body. When I move, my blood moves faster. Calories are consumed, and energy results in my body radiating heat and the energy of my physical life force.

Air—Breath, speech, chanting, singing. In ritual, I add Air when I participate by speaking aloud an intention or wish, when I lend my voice to the chant. When we sing together, we are breathing together, harmonizing our breaths and our pulses. We don't need to be good singers to still make a sound and add the energy of our voice.

Fire—Rhythm, percussion, drumming. Drummers can add some of the intense sound and rhythm to the ritual. I can also add rhythm by clapping, stamping, snapping my fingers, or through vocal percussion and making rhythmic sounds with my mouth.

Water—Connection, intention, emotion. I can connect to the intention of the ritual within the depth of my heart, and to others in the ritual through deep, sustained eye contact or through touching hands. If I'm emotionally invested in the intention, in the community, if I'm connecting to the divine and to the divine within me, then I am adding my emotional energy to the ritual. If I can't physically or rhythmically engage, if I'm not comfortable singing, I can add my energy by holding the intention in my heart.

Energy Flow
Any ritual has an energetic flow, and what happens in the first few minutes of the ritual will set the tone for later on. In the rituals I offer, which are in the ecstatic tradition taught through Reclaiming, Diana's Grove, and other shamanic traditions, I am working to get people engaged in the ritual and inviting participation.

Here is a typical flow of a public ritual in the style I use. Usually these rituals are facilitated by an ensemble team. Each piece may have more than one person leading it.

- **Marketing/promotion:** Emails and flyers set the tone for the ritual theme and helps build communal trust in the ritual team.

- **Arrivals/Greeting:** As people come to the space, the ritual team works to greet the participants. Ideally everything's already set up so that we can welcome people to the space, since welcoming makes people feel more safe, and thusly, more willing to risk singing and moving later. Having social time of at least a half hour before the ritual helps people transition from interacting with traffic into ritual space.

- **Pre-Ritual Talk:** This session (15 minutes or less to hold people's attention) addresses the theme, intention, and any ritual logistics. Give people a chance to speak, even if it's going around the circle with names, as that sets a tone of participation and helps the group move from strangers into a tribe. It's a good time to address basic group agreements of what's ok to do and to teach any chants so that people aren't stumbling to learn them later. Typically I will also use the elemental model (above) to let people know how they can add their energy.

- **Gathering:** Instead of beginning with smudging or similar purifications that involve a long line, Diana's Grove uses an energetic gathering. This is somewhat a purification of sound and rhythm as well as a way to get people from individual mind into group mind. The idea is to begin at the energetic level of where the group is and take them to a more collective place. You can have the group sing a tone, or you can get people clapping and moving and singing to build up some energetic fuel for later in the ritual.

- **Grounding:** As much as the gathering is energetic and group mind, grounding, in this context, is about connecting more deeply to myself, becoming more present to the divine, and connecting to the theme of the work. A typical tree grounding can work just fine, or any meditation to facilitate participants going internal to get into a sacred mindset.

- **Casting a Circle:** For the rituals I offer, casting a circle is less about an energetic barrier keeping negative energies out, and more about an energetic boundary acknowledging that we are here together as a tribe. As grounding is internal, circle casting takes us out of ourselves to connect as a tribe.

The circle is the edge of our tribe for the ritual, and it's important to establish connection and safety. This is the cauldron that will hold the soup. In ecstatic participatory ritual, one or two people facilitate the circle casting but the intention is to have participants add their energy to the process. The challenge is to do an inclusive casting, or invocation, in around 2 minutes or less to keep people engaged.

- **Invoking the Elements:** The elemental invocations, similarly, are an opportunity to invite participants to lend their voice, body, movement, and intention, as well as to deepen the theme. In the rituals I work in, instead of facing the direction, the elemental invoker moves into the center and facilitates a process where the whole group invokes the element. An example: "Will you join me in welcoming Air? Will you take a breath together, will you make the sound that is the wind in the trees that blows the leaves to the ground, will you move as air moves? Air is the breath of life, can you feel how the change in the air heralds the change in the seasons? Welcome Air."

- **Center:** I typically work with center as the gravity well that draws the community together. What is the reason that people came? This is another opportunity to connect the group together as a tribe, and to the center that holds us.

- **Deities, ancestors, allies:** We invite in whichever deities or allies we'll be working with in as inclusive a way as possible. What each person participates in is more potent than them watching a ritualist do something. Liturgy and poetry can be powerful, but if you want the group to add their energy later on, give them some way to participate in every piece, even if it's just closing their eyes and imagining the ancestors.

- **Storytelling:** Often the working part of the ritual begins with storytelling or some piece to add context to what we're doing in the ritual. This piece can be longer than 2 minutes, provided people are given a chance to get comfortable.

- **Trance Journey:** Storytelling often transitions into a trance journey which takes the theme of the story and move it from a story about gods and heroes into a story that we personally can interact in. Storytelling, and trance journeys, brings people's energy internal and will require a transition if I want them to come out of trance and be active.

- **Physicalization:** As much as possible, it helps to offer experiences for multiple learning styles (visual, auditory, kinesthetic, etc.). If the trance journey took us to a place where we connect with the fire of our personal magic, then the physicalization might be inviting people to choose a stone to represent their magic. Or it might be to have them stand and go to an altar and offer their personal magic to Brigid's forge to be transformed. A physicalization helps integrate the ritual intention, as well as transitions people from internal to external so they are more ready to participate in the energy.

- **Energy Building:** A sustained energy piece is the fuel for the magic. Often it helps to start slow and build through layering chanting, movement, harmonies, vocal percussion, drumming, and more. The ritualist team should be fully engaged; if you aren't willing to stand up and sing, no one else will be. The energy may rise to a peak of sound and rhythm, and after there is usually a moment of silence. A typical time length for energy is 8-10 minutes; 15 minutes may be longer than many people can chant. The energy, and the ritual, should have a defined ending. People can drum and dance more after ritual.

- **Benediction:** Let people know what the ritual was about, such as, "Brigid, thank you for helping us find our personal magic and transform it in your forge. May we support each other in community." This seals the deal on the working and leads to devoking the allies and elements. Opening the circle is a last chance for the group to connect as a tribe before opening.

- **Dessert/Feast:** Ecstatic participatory rituals tend to not use cakes and ale within the ceremony because of the energetic lag created by a long wait for food to be passed around. Post-ritual dessert or feasting is an intentional bonding time to grow community.

Layering the Energy
To build up a sustained energy, it helps to layer in voice, rhythm, and movement. As each layer builds, gently bring in another layer, as that will feel more natural to the group and they will be more likely to participate. Drummers should follow the group's energy rather than drive the group; building it too fast and the group may "check out." If the energy spikes up too fast you can drop the chant down to a whisper and build it back up. You can invite group participation through eye contact, beckoning, or by asking, "Will you join your movement and voice to this ritual?"

Having a team of people willing to sing and dance models what behavior is "ok" to the group and creates safety. Watch a ritual where one person starts to clap; if no one else does, they'll stop. But if a second or third person does, then others will.

If you have some strong singers, you can use a chant with 2 parts or harmonies to add another layer of energy. A basket of rhythm instruments is another opportunity for people to add a sound.

Working the energy is a balance of letting the group drive how fast the chant builds, and pushing the energy along. The energy will plateau, and rise again when you add a layer. At first it's hard to sense if the group's ready to be done, or if it's just a natural plateau where another layer will build the energy back up.

Noticing Energy
Begin to take more notice of people's body language. Are these people willing to stand up and sing? The kinds of energy you can build in ritual will depend on your team—do you have drummers and singers? How many attendees—10 or 100? What's the chant you are using—is it cradling, or an energy-raiser?

Observe the rituals of different groups. What happens to the energy when 40 people smudge themselves or stand in line at an altar? How long do people speak? When is it boring? When are people invigorated, willing to sing or participate? When are glazed over?

While the skill set of building ecstatic energy in ritual takes time and practice, these tools should offer a way to frame ritual in terms of energy and begin to build techniques into your own rituals. With practice, you can raise the sacred fire of ecstatic energy in your rituals.

This article is published in Stepping Into Ourselves: An Anthology of Writing About Priestesses, which is an amazing resource for anyone involved in Pagan leadership and ritual facilitation. http://www.goddess-ink.com/priestessanthology.html

Reasons to Raise Energy

When do you raise energy in rituals? Why do you raise energy? And what do you do with the energy you've raised? What happens in a ritual when big energy is raised and nothing's done with it?

I think with any ritual, so much is based upon the intention of the ritual work. And rituals rarely have just one intention. Is the ritual to do an act of magic, to honor the gods, to acknowledge the season, to do personal growth/transformative work, to build community, to acknowledge a rite of passage, to facilitate a grieving process? Likely it's a combination of things.

When building or raising energy, the team of people facilitating the ritual needs to look at the intention of the ritual and match any energy work being done with that intention. For instance, if the ritual is solely about personal transformative work, then I could offer a ritual structured to get people into a personal trance state to do their own work. Energy would be raised but the room might be darker and people would be encouraged to have their eyes closed or half-lidded to facilitate the privacy of personal work done in a communal setting.

On the other hand, if the ritual is intended to build community, then I'm going to want enough light so that people can meet each other's eyes. If I want to build community, people need to at least see each other to connect with one another. I would encourage the people singing and moving to do the energy building with their eyes opened at least part of the time. They wouldn't just having their own experience but sharing that energy—sharing at least some aspect of themselves--with others.

If the intention of the ritual is to make space for grieving, then the energy wouldn't necessarily be a "cone of power," but perhaps a rocking/cradling chant, or a ritualist offering an invocation, poem, or trance journey that takes people into a deep emotional place. I've facilitated rituals where there was deep crying and grieving, with people literally on the floor uttering terrible things that had happened to them, and that raised more energy than many "cones of power" in other rituals.

Energy doesn't have to be loud to be intense.

What's the Goal?
But the question comes back to, why is that energy being raised (or moved, or transformed) and what is being done with it? In a grief ritual, I think the goal is a release, a catharsis, and a transformation into hope for the future. In a ritual where a magical act is being done--casting a spell, or sending energy to a particular political goal or effort--there's a clear focus.

I've done an energy raising as part of an ADF Druidry ritual where we did ecstatic work (singing, moving) to hallow the blessing (waters which people would drink in to drink in the blessing of the gods). There was a visual focus--the water, and an auditory focus--the chant, as well other focuses (shared movement, dance).

Some rituals I've seen that fall into the Chaos Magic/Occult realm, or other rituals that are more reconstructionist traditions, or African Diasporic traditions, such as Seidhr rituals or Vodou, the energy that is raised by the group is channeled into one person who aspects/draws down a deity into themselves.

It's sometimes more difficult to channel the energy to a specific focus when the intention is personal growth work. That energy is occasionally more like shooting the energy up to the ceiling and letting it fall like rain, or something more like drinking the heated waters of a cauldron. In fact, when I'm building energy like that I try to shape the group less like a cone, and more like a cauldron, where we're cooking in the energy, and the energy is the spiritual heat/fire that effects the transformation.

What if There's no Focus?

I believe that, even without a clear focus and channeling of the energy, the energy goes where it's needed. I believe that even the act of engaging in an ecstatic ritual and raising that energy can effect a transformation—that energy runs through our bodies and changes us for the better. We don't always know what we're praying for-- sometimes we're just praying for things to be better, we're praying for an unnamed blessing, and the energy goes where it's needed. And even moving that kind of energy through our bodies can shake up our old patterns and transform us.

Typically when I'm offering a public ritual, one of my intentions is community building. Many of the people attending my rituals have never been to a ritual before, or haven't been involved with the Pagan community at all. In some ways, the ecstatic energy raising becomes a "carrot" to get them involved again.

The trick to this carrot is, the energy raising feels good and people like it, and for some maybe it becomes just an endorphin high. However, I've found that the more I engage with it in a specific group, it transcends being just about the endorphin high of running that kind of energy and 100 people pounding out a chant on the floor.

Over time, that energy (with the intention to do this) can build community. It's tricky. I have to begin slowly, get people to actually acknowledge each other and look into each other's eyes. If I can get them to do that, maybe I can get them to whisper their dream for the future to one another, or even say it aloud into the center.

For a group of people that doesn't know each other, that's a big step. It's a lot more intimacy than they were perhaps prepared for when they walked in to a public ritual, but usually they're thanking me after.

Energy Builds Community
What happens after the energy building is interesting. There is a sort of ambient energy to the room—to the group. People have shared something together, and that energy keeps on simmering. After a big energy-raising ritual, people have something to talk about.

In essence, the ice is broken.

Some of you may disagree with this—and I acknowledge that this comes from my perspective as a Pantheist. But sometimes I think that the point of a ritual with community building as one of the intentions may have less to do with honoring the seasons and the gods and more to do with giving people enough energy to actually be social with each other. Having gone through that ritual, they have something to talk about, and I have seen that ritual energy become the icebreaker that builds lasting friendships and stronger communities..

It is the friendship and tribe energy that builds the foundation of a community, it's connection that keeps people coming back. I can offer great rituals, with lots of endorphin-pumping energy, but if people don't leave with some kind of personal connection, they usually don't make a point of coming back.

The big energy-raising rituals can focus that energy--still provide the peak experience, but also use it for a purpose.

Ecstatic Ritual
In the rituals I facilitate, I'm using ecstatic practices including participation. It's not just about me facilitating an experience for a group, it's me trying to help that group facilitate the experience for themselves. Over time, this energetic builds volunteers and joiners, vs. audiences who watch but don't have a stake.

Instead of just invoking something with my own poetry, I'd step into the center and ask people to imagine what's important to them about the (element/ancestor/deity/etc.) and to perhaps speak that aloud. That invests their energy and emotion in the ritual. If they're invested, vs. just watching me do something, and I can build that investment over time, they're more likely to feel a connection to the work and feel that they can participate and be involved.

As I almost always say before I offer a public ritual, we each bring the energy to this ritual. I can't raise the energy in the ritual without you. What if we each sang and danced and breathed and moved and concentrated like it mattered, like this ritual really mattered?

It's a shift in perspective but it leads to a different kind of energy. Not just the spiky "Hey we build a cone and that was fun!" kind of energy, but a deeper, "We're connected and raising this energy for a shared purpose" energy.

Whenever you're working to build energy, think about what your intention is. Why are you building that energy? What is being done with it? How are you building it, and how are people joining in?

By focusing on your intention, your ritual will not only have a greater chance at success, but you'll also have an easier time figuring out how to facilitate that part of your ritual.

Ritual Design & Facilitation: Ritual Bling and Magical Mood-Setting

First published in CIRCLE Magazine issue 114

Once upon a time I facilitated a ritual in Chicago and was quoted by a journalist covering his first Pagan ritual. Unfortunately, the quote he chose was when I said, "It's all about the bling." Fortunately he didn't quote me by name or that would have been really embarrassing. Ultimately, the article was actually fairly positive; the slightly out-of-context quote was actually me laughing with other ritualists as I was setting up the central altar for the evening's ritual.

I have jokingly referred to my large collection of altar decorations and outfits as "ritual bling."

If you've been to one of my rituals or seen my Facebook photo albums, you've probably seen some of the elaborate altars and other visual setups that I create. In fact, my van is a mobile storage unit for the massive amount of ritual bling I use. I also regularly offer extra gowns, robes, swaths of fabric, or scarves and stoles to people taking ritual roles who don't have their own ritual-wear. Setup is time consuming; I can't tell you how many hours of my life have been spent hauling bins of supplies.

Why Bother With All that Bling?
People do ask me that. What people ask me more frequently is, "But…how did you get us all dancing and singing and crying? How can I do that?"

My first suggestion is usually to light a fire or candles. But what does lighting a bonfire or candles have to do with chanting? What do altar setups and ritual clothing really have to do with a successful ritual?

In the end, they are all set dressings; we don't really need them. But we humans are creatures of habit, and these trappings help us to suspend our sense of disbelief. We get bound up in cultural expectations of how to act. It's not ok to dance or sing, to have an emotion in front of people in public. That's embarrassing, don't do that, people will laugh.

Creating a ritual that takes us to a deeply intimate place of connection to the divine, to each other, to our highest self, is a tremendous challenge. Getting a group of people who don't know each other to be ok with dancing, singing, and expressing sorrow or joy or other real emotions, means getting people to lay aside societal expectations.

In my experience, this is the hardest part of effecting actual meaningful, magical, potent rituals—helping people to get over themselves and stop worrying they are going to look stupid.

Suspending Disbelief

I use many and varied techniques to help people open up, feel safe, and be willing to risk emotion. I'm trying to take people out of the everyday; it's difficult for a participant in a ritual to connect to deep magic when there are reminders of the modern world all around.

Glaring fluorescent lights, T-shirts with slogans, tennis shoes, posters and advertisements, cars driving by...all of these serve to bring us back to the fact that we're a bunch of folks dancing around looking ridiculous.

And our ego does not want us to look ridiculous.

When I create elaborate altars, draped fabric archways, or alcoves, I'm trying to destroy that sense of the modern and the societal constraints of don't laugh, don't sing, don't cry, don't dance, don't embarrass yourself. Similarly, I try to dress in a way that removes as much of the modern as I can. I opt for long gowns in jewel tone colors, a scarf around my neck, sometimes a sleeveless duster/robe. I keep my glasses on for necessity, but even those I'll take off if I feel it will help take the group deeper.

I ask people taking ritual roles in my rituals to not wear any overtly modern clothing. Modern shoes, collared shirts, t-shirts, shirts with words or logos, any of these will take the participants out of the magic.

But I Don't Have Bling

Even without a closet full of ritual wear, there are ways you can adapt your clothing to help people stay in "the zone." A sweater and jeans can work with a simple duster or long scarf

Similarly, I don't advocate overdressing. Renaissance Faire costumes or overly elaborate outfits can be distracting. I've made the mistake of wearing overly-complicated costumes and ended up tripping on the fabric--definitely less-than-magical! On occasion intricate outfits can work, such as if someone is drawing down a particular deity, but be sure that you aren't going to be in danger of trailing bits of fabric catching on fire.

You're not trying to overwhelm people with your flashy gear; you're helping participants to understand on a nonverbal level that you're a professional who's helping take them between the worlds.

How Do I Build Up My Collection?
Many of my ritual clothes have come from thrift stores, or I've sewed them myself. I've also hand-dyed rayon dresses from Dharma Trading, a technique I learned at Diana's Grove.

For altars, I collect pieces such as elemental-colored candle holders, bowls, and fabric to drape over tables. I hunt pieces out at thrift stores, Home Goods, Hobby Lobby, Michaels, JoAnn's, or other places where you can get decorative items. Christmastime, or clearance aisles, get great deals. Craigslist.com can be a place to check, as brides often sell off elaborate decorations from weddings. I try to buy fabric in pieces at least 3 yards in length as that is enough to cover most tables, and use smaller decorative fabric as the centerpiece of an altar.

In the photos here, and in the color photos in my Facebook photo albums, I make the pieces in the center higher with cake stands or fabric-draped boxes. Shorter items go on the sides. I rarely use statues, but those could be placed in the center of an altar and given more presence and focus by being placed on a higher stand. I also collect small mirrors, which add dimension and depth to altars.

Large decorative altars, arbors, draped fabric, and fire will instantly begin to take people into the magic. The colors are engaging, the shiny pieces glisten, and people begin to wonder, what is the magic we will join in tonight?

Candles

I have over a hundred votive holders. Even without all the other bins of supplies, you can evoke a magical mood with a hundred shimmering tealights. You can get small glass votives inexpensively at thrift stores; they don't have to match.

Something I have also done is saved all my glass pasta and pickle jars. I clean them and use Goo-Gone to remove adhesive labels. Then I have a tall, sturdy tealight holder that can be placed on the floor and participants are unlikely to have a skirt catch fire. Use the long butane lighters or long matches to light these.

Cauldron Fire

I'd say if there's one ritual supply investment that's worth more than all the other pretty bits, it's a cauldron. An indoor cauldron fire is a technique that I use at almost every ritual. Cast iron is best. A bowling-ball size cauldron will cost $30-$50. I have a brass cauldron that I thrifted for $5, but you should always do a test burn before ritual; some metal can't hold up to the heat.

Fill your cauldron within an inch or two from the top with Epsom salts, then fill it with rubbing alcohol until the alcohol is floating just above the salt. Light it with a taper candle, or a long-stem match—a butane lighter in the middle of ritual will bring people back to the modern. The fire burns for 15-45 minutes, depending on the size and how much alcohol you pour.

The alcohol burns almost without smoke; I've never had this set off a smoke detector, and it doesn't bother my throat when I'm singing. It's also a fairly safe fire; it's fairly difficult for someone to actually catch fire from this.

Typically, I place the cauldron on a low central altar where it becomes the Axis Mundi, the center that we gather around. Keeping the fire low means we can get in close it and have enough light to see each others' eyes across the fire.

Facilitation is More Challenging Without Mood

To put a mathematical value on bling, I can honestly say I have to work twice as hard to get a group chanting if I don't have a fire. If it's a bright room or daylight, double that. The hardest rituals for me to facilitate and get a group to open up are at events like Pagan Pride. It's bright daylight, no candles, no fire, cars are zooming by, there are curious people watching, there's a soccer game going on next door...there's an endless list of distractions and reminders that we all look ridiculous.

When I'm facilitating rituals at a hotel conference that doesn't allow fire, I dim the lights. Sometimes mood lighting is all you have access to, and it can be enough to take people into "the zone." At times I've used LED candles; I recommend the amber ones in semi-opaque votive holders as they look more realistic. The expensive fake pillar candle ones look even better.

RITUAL FACILITATION

Care with Settings

If you're trying to get ritual participants to a deeper, more magical place, take extra effort with your physical/mundane setting to support that.

You might to find a ritual spot that is bordered at least partially by trees. People will feel a little safer, plus you get sound containment for chanting. Consider dressing to set mood without being ostentatious. A simple black or elemental-colored gown or tunic, a nice scarf, a simple duster, can bring a formality and focus to your presence. It really will help people to forget about the cars and soccer game.

Consider investing in some decorations to help people focus. Sometimes I don't even physically use the altars during the ritual, they are just there to hold a visual/kinesthetic presence, such as elemental or deity altars.

Even without decorations, you can invite people to remove their shoes, silence their cell phones. It's also important to remove some of the jarringly modern elements from the room/ritual area. Asking people to move purses and backpacks to an unobtrusive area, lowering lights, bringing in floorlamps to avoid using overheads, can transform a room completely. If there are posters up on the walls, or tables and chairs in the way, or plastic bags or other overtly modern clutter, try to open up the space, remove the visual distractions.

Language and Words Set the Mood

Beyond all the trappings of outfits and decorations, you can engage a timeless space through language. Bling is actually a word I'd never use in a ritual; it's too modern. However, generally ideophones or onomatopoeia are good choices for evocative ritual language.

> *"Bling (or bling-bling) is a slang term...referring to flashy, ostentatious or elaborate jewelry and ornamented accessories....In linguistics terms, bling is an ideophone intended to evoke the "sound" of light hitting silver, platinum, or diamonds. It is not an onomatopoeia, because the act of jewelry shining does not make a sound."*
> http://en.wikipedia.org/wiki/Bling-bling

Open, accessible language that takes people out of time is a topic for a future article, but consider these words and how they make you feel: Formeldahyde, Minivan, Facebook, jurisdiction, alarm clock, getting in the car, pants.

Do any of these help you feel more magical? Probably not. Here's a few more words: Journeying, splashing, transformation, center, brother, breath, green, timepiece, garment.

Can you sense the difference? I'm not advocating talking like you're at Ren Faire, but finding words that are simple, elegant, and less modern, help to craft a timeless space. Generally, words that are more Anglo-Saxon have more onomatopoeia and speak more to our deep self. Mother, father, brother, sister, are more magical sounding than parent or sibling.

Bring the Magic
How can your space promote safety and comfort for your participants? What artwork or decorations would help take people out of time? What clothing helps to serve ritual intention, and what is distracting? Are you able to work with fire or lower the lights? What words will help evoke a space between the worlds?

Ritual Design & Facilitation: Managing Complicated Logistics

First published in CIRCLE Magazine Issue 117

Physical logistics in ritual refer to when people get up and do a thing. Engaging physical participation is one of the most effective ways to engage your group. Unfortunately, it's also the area of ritual that's most often rife with disaster. Poorly-handled ritual logistics is easily the fastest way to lose the energy and focus of your group.

It's also the most common ritual facilitation mistake I see.

I pick on Cakes and Ale a lot, as well as smudging/saging, but both are the two most common offenders. Theoretically, both involve multiple senses, which is a great way to engage your participants. Having people participate deepens their experience. However, I remember the last time I was at a Cakes and Ale at an 80 person ritual. Even with four people handing out cups, pouring juice, handing out cookies, it was still boring. People started chatting.

Sage and incense can take forever too; in my book "Spiritual Scents" I talk about a 60-person ritual where just the smudging took 45 minutes. That's too long.

People ask me all the time how they can make their rituals better, and engaging participation is definitely the way to go. There are some key facilitation techniques that can help manage these logistics. A lot of it is planning and actually walking through it so you know how long it will take and so you can adjust your ritual accordingly.

Scenario: Fall Harvest
My favorite emails are when people ask me, "So I'm doing this ritual and...." One ritualist asked me for help with a harvest ritual. She wanted two large scarecrow effigies of the God and Goddess where participants could make an offering.

Challenges:
- Getting people moving in the first place
- One-on-one interaction with the God/Goddess (Scarecrows) could take forever...everyone gets bored
- People getting cold
- Enough light to see

The Space
How you handle these logistics at an indoor venue would differ greatly from an outdoor ritual; check out the layout of the space. Your logistics are different if your Scarecrow/Effigies are in the center of the circle vs. to one side. Let's assume outdoors, with effigies to the side.

Lighting and Warmth
This is easily resolved with a central bonfire. Then the key is to provide enough lighting at the edge of the space, and ensure that

participants are spending most of their time close to the fire and not standing to the side in the cold.

Tiki torches are good for border lighting. I often use votive candles on tables to the side for indoor venues. Pro tip: Taper candles and pillars have a tendency to get knocked over, staining altar-cloths in wax and singing ritual outfits. A few tiki torches near the Effigies, or 20-30 tealights in glass will throw focus to the area and help participants to see what's going on.

This is Taking Forever!
This is usually the most challenging part to skillfully facilitate. But there are many ways to keep things moving.

Chant to Hold Space
A simple chant that is themed to the mood you're going for helps hold people's attention. Chanting is a powerful way to sink a group into a trance state; check out my article on Chanting in CIRCLE Magazine issue 115 or in the "Stepping Into Ourselves" anthology from Goddess Ink. You can also join my Chants and Chanting Facebook group for more resources.

Tell the Group What You Want
Do a pre-ritual talk. Before the actual ritual starts, tell people what effect you're going for in the ritual and what you'd like to happen. You can do it right before ritual, or make a few announcements before/after a mealtime; any time most ritual attendees are gathered.

I might say something like, "In tonight's ritual, each person will have an opportunity to go to the Goddess and God, in the form of the Harvest Scarecrows, to make an offering."

You should physically gesture to where the Effigies are so people know 1. Where they physically are and 2. What they symbolize

"After _____ in the ritual, we'll begin singing the chant _____, and then people can process to the Goddess and God to make your offerings."

Manage Types of Offerings

There's a vast difference between people offering a word or prayer, or asking them to bring an offering, or having a bowl full of some object for them to take and then offer. If people are expected to bring something with them, they need to know that far ahead of time, especially if it's something that will be released and burned.

If you're giving participants offering supplies, then you have to plan the logistics of how to get those offerings into their hands without adding yet another long line. You also need to give people time to spiritually connect to what they are offering. However, these can go hand in hand quite well.

Perhaps you have a bowl of grains, and each person can take a handful. And when they make the offering, they are supposed to speak (or hold the silent intention) of something they've harvested this year.

So you need to have enough bowls of grains to make it easy for everyone to get their offering without waiting in line. You also need to offer a reflective/trance/meditation opportunity for them to identify what that thing is first. Nothing frustrates people more than being suddenly asked, "What has your harvest been this year," or, "What do you offer to the divine," without a chance to think on it. It's especially important to give adequate preparation time for your long-processors. Short-processors tend to have answers on the tip of their tongue. Other folks need more time.

What's great is that the very act of offering a meditation/trance on what that offering is can fill the time while the seeds are being passed out so that people won't even notice they are "standing in line."

During your pre-ritual talk, ask some of those questions so people can start mulling on it. "Begin to think of what you might offer to the God and Goddess. What do you leave there with them, what do you sacrifice? As the grain is sacrificed for us to eat, what do we offer back in return?" or, "To the God and Goddess of harvest, what do you offer? Is there something you have accomplished this year that you wish to dedicate to Them?" Give people something specific to energetically focus on for their offering.

Really, Ask For What You Want
It's ok to tell people they need to hurry up, though there's better ways to say it. You might try:

> "At the point in the ritual when we begin to sing the chant, you are invited to approach the God and Goddess and make your offering. More than one person can make an offering at the same time; there is room for three or four of you at once. I also ask that you keep things moving to respect the needs of the others around you.
>
> "If you find you need more than just a few moments with the God and the Goddess, you are welcome to step to the side to continue your personal devotional work, just please allow other folks in the ritual to come forward to make their own offerings. We have sixty people here. If each person took a minute, we'd be waiting for an hour. There will also be time after the ritual if you need to do further work with them."

The specifics depend greatly on your ritual, but outlining your expectations clearly will ensure that they are met. I attended a Winter Solstice ritual where each person lit a votive candle off the person next to them then spoke an intention. Nobody placed a time limit. Sixty people sitting on a cold floor…it took an hour and a half. My back was in agony. It's really ok to say, "We have sixty people here, so please speak an intention in just a few words, perhaps a sentence." You can point out, "If each person took thirty seconds, we'd be here for a half hour. Please be considerate of the group."

If you don't ask for it, you won't get it. In fact, giving people a heads up and asking them to be considerate with how much time they take—and giving them a metric--will solve about half of your logistical problems. This is crucial to do before—not during—the ritual. It's a really awkward transition if done during the ritual.

When you let people know what the specific parameter is, they'll usually follow it. "Keep it brief" is a good start, but the word is subjective. "Keep it to three words or a sentence" is more specific.

If the group isn't keeping things brief during the ritual itself, it's all right to offer a subtle reminder. "And as you approach the God and the Goddess, making your offering with brevity and solemnity and returning to the fire," or if people start lining up and then doing one-at-a-time at the altar, "The God and Goddess can listen to many voices. Come forward," gesturing so that 3-4 people come forward at once.

Keeping Things Moving
You'll want to establish several support roles. Some call these folks "plants" or "schills." I call them leaders.

A crucial role that is often overlooked is "modeling." Have several people designated to go first and "model" the behavior you want the group to follow. In this case, you'll want people walking around with the bowls of seeds, and you'll want everyone on your ritual team to model taking a handful of seeds smoothly and quickly—not rushing, but not taking forever. You'd be surprised how people slowly taking handfuls of things out of a bowl slows the process down.

Similarly, when the chant begins and it's time to begin processing to the God/Goddess effigies, several leaders can go and model :

- How this can be done in under 20 seconds while keeping a sacred mood,
- How three people can simultaneously visit effigies without disturbing each other,
- How to move to the side and make space for others.

People will follow the leader. If the first person out takes forever in front of the effigy, everyone else will feel like they have to hang out there and contemplate for a really long time in order to look like they're "doing it right." Remember, in ritual, we're often in a trance. People can obsess over silly things. This is particularly true of people who are unsure and new to ritual.

Depending upon your group you might want to have two "anchors" near the Effigies/altar. These are people who would stand quietly to the side, and if someone is taking more than a minute, they might gently approach and invite the person over to the side to continue their communion with the God/Goddess, but still make room for other participants to come forward.

I often put people in this role in a veil. It helps offer them a gentle but firm presence. Make sure they aren't being ritual enforcers; this is a gentle, loving invitation to help the seeker continue their work yet keep things moving.

Do the Math
How long does each logistic take, per person? Yes...Ritual Algebra! Actually, the math is pretty simple. If you have 60 people, 3 people simultaneously taking one minute is 20 minutes. That's a long time to stand and sustain a chant, particularly out in the cold. Three people taking 30 seconds is 10 minutes. That's better. Three people taking 20 seconds is a bit shorter than that. 4 people at the effigies at once taking about 20 seconds would be less than 5 minutes. Bingo.

The important thing with doing the math is, you have to know how long something actually takes, not how long you want it to take.

I bet the ritual facilitator at that Winter Solstice ritual didn't count out how long it takes to light one tealight off of another. But I counted. Over and over--nearly 20 seconds. It's difficult to light them off of each other. Also, when people are asked to light a candle and then speak an intention, they almost always take a deep meaningful pause to gaze at the candle, which can add 5-10 seconds.

Is all this math ridiculous? Well, just between lighting the candles and gazing, we're talking 20-30 seconds per attendee, and they haven't even spoken their intention yet. While that moment of speaking is full of intention and energy for that one person, everyone else is getting more and more bored.

Give People Something To Do
People won't realize they are waiting if they are busy. On the rare occasions when I have people stand in line at an altar, I usually have them singing a chant, or, I have people facilitating a trance journey asking them meaningful questions pertinent to the ritual working at hand.

In the case of the example we've been working with, when people finish leaving their offering and speaking to the God/Goddess, you might invite them to return to the fire. The chant can hold that focus and intention. If you're using a trance journey/meditation that is facilitated simultaneously while people approach the Effigies, you can invite them to gaze into the fire and reflect on the past year and what they've harvested, what they've learned, what they must release.

Without a focus, people will start to chitchat. Inviting them closer to the fire ensures that people stay warm.

Avoiding Train Wrecks

It seems so simple when you start planning your ritual. But you can see probably a dozen places where that ritual could turn into a boring three-hour-tour. What's most important is to think through and walk through the ritual. Find places where things could go wrong and adapt your design.

Ritual Design & Facilitation: Accessibility, Learning Modalities, and Logistics

It seems so simple when you start planning your ritual. "We'll have everyone walk to _____. " Yet there are many ways where a physical logistic can cause a ritual train wreck. Any ritual plan also raises considerable issues around working with physical accessibility and different learning modalities. Some of your attendees may not be able to stand throughout the whole ritual, and some cannot walk at all. Some may be blind or deaf. Some may learn better kinesthetically, others visually.

In previous articles I've written about designing rituals that flow to prevent a "three hour tour," and I've also written a little about engaging different learning modalities, but here we'll go into a little more depth.

Part of my values include making ritual as accessible and inclusive as possible. While sometimes there are considerable constraints on what I'm able to do including location and budget, there are lots of ways to make people feel welcome and to help people with varying learning modalities engage fully in your ritual.

Unintentionally Dogmatic Pagan Practices
Most rituals I attend make almost no accommodations for people's differing physical needs. The most dogmatic practice I witness is expecting everyone to stand throughout an entire ritual. Most rituals I attend are pretty talky, and only addressing people who respond best to auditory learning. There's also the expectation that everyone is fine with having sage waved in their face.

When I first offered public rituals I knew some ways to be inclusive. I knew to tell people that they could sit if they needed to, but then came the day where literally half of the group was unable to participate in walking to different altars/stations. I thought, "What do I do now?" I was able to adapt and offer a trance journey version of the experience, but I was not prepared for that.

Inclusivity and Accessibility
Inclusion is both inviting participation as well as ensuring that people actually feel welcome at your ritual. One sure-fire way to ensure that participants don't have a deep spiritual experience is to exclude them by your language or physical assumptions.

Sometimes your ritual location is what it is; your group does rituals in a forest preserve, or, the only space you can afford to rent is up a flight of stairs. However, if your ritual is intended to be accessible, then you must take that into account when designing your event.

This includes the venue you rent to how you set up your space to how you use language. If you ask people to stand and journey to a place of power through a walking trance, do you also offer an experience for those who can't walk? Are you offering more than just a visualization for those who cannot see, or who aren't primarily visual? You may not be able to afford an interpreter, but have you made sure that a deaf participant can see the ritual facilitators to read their lips? Incense is an amazing spiritual anchor for some, and a direct road to an asthma attack for others.

Explore what logistics cause difficulty by looking at your entire ritual process through space setup, logistics, and language use.

Accessibility: Physical Mobility
Bad knees, fibromyalgia, back pain, arthritis. Some people will have a hard time standing during rituals. I try to choose a ritual venues that are accessible; think about stairs, long hikes through the woods, even public transportation…make a list. I also try to ensure that people in my ritual are empowered to sit. I'm amazed at how many rituals go on and on, and people with canes in obvious discomfort do their best to stand through a ritual because nobody offered them the choice to sit.

During my pre-ritual talk, I outline a few agreements such as, "I will invite people to stand, move, and sing, and if you need to sit down you are welcome to do so. Participate as much as you are physically able. If you need to bring a chair in please ask someone's help."

There are more ways to include people with different physical needs than I can outline here, but the key is to think out your plan ahead of time and look at the different accessibility issues you face.

Spiral Dance Pro-Tip: Sometimes people end up stumbling all over each other, or people's arms get stretched out painfully if they are led too quickly, or they are on uneven ground. Allow people who can't walk it to pull chairs into the center facing out—they can still participate in the eye-contact portion of the dance.

Accessibility: Scent, Incense, Sage, and other Smoke
I've talked to many Pagans who are baffled when I suggest that I do not purify with sage. I personally facilitate almost all of my rituals without smoking/scented things. I, and many other Pagans, are

allergic and sensitive to sage, incense, smoke, essential oils, perfumes, and more.

In fact, I get the question so often that I wrote a short eBook on the topic, **"Spiritual Scents,"** on how to use scent appropriately, and how to facilitate potent rituals without using any scent, smoke, or fire. I personally would love to attend more rituals where I'm not struggling to breathe and my face isn't itching.

It should go without saying (but, I often have to say it) that anyone smoking should not do so indoors, or near the main ritual area, during the ritual, or too close to the doors.

Ritual for Multiple Learning Modalities
Who will be at your ritual? Gregarious folks, shy folks...people who learn best through spoken words, or through music, or through movement. In short, everyone will be there. So your job as a facilitator is to design a ritual that hits many different modalities.

Understanding learning modalities and multiple intelligences will open up a whole new world for you as far as getting people into a headspace where they can actually do the deep work of connecting to the divine. Learning how to do this artfully is an incredible skill that will serve any work you are doing in offering community ritual.

- **Learning Modalities:** Auditory, Kinesthetic, Visual, and sometimes Emotional
- **Multiple Intelligences:** Taking that further, there's visual-spatial, verbal-linguistic, logical-mathematical, bodily-kinesthetic, musical-rhythmic, interpersonal, intrapersonal, and naturalistic.
- **Other Polarities:** I learned to work with several polarities after hearing someone talk about a few techniques of Neuro-Linguistic Programming (NLP). Here are some common ones I work with: introverts/extroverts, internal

processors/external processors, long-processors/short processors, and reachers-for/movers-away-from.

I was introduced to learning modalities and multiple intelligences at Diana's Grove, particularly by Dr. L Carol Scott and Jennifer Wilson, but it was a core value embedded into the Diana's Grove ritual style. I was introduced to what I call the polarities just by picking things up from various folks talking about NLP. The theory of multiple intelligences comes from Howard Gardner in his book "Frames of Mind" though you can also figure out the basics on http://en.wikipedia.org/wiki/Multiple_intelligences or by doing a web search and reading articles on the topic.

The idea is that we all have different ways of learning, different preferences for how we engage with the world. Some of us learn best visually, others verbally, others kinesthetically, others emotionally. Typically, we have a dominant learning modality.

Learning Modalities and Trance
Making things more complex, our least-dominant learning modality is often how we engage in a trance state. I get into the deepest trances through music. There's a book on working with learning modalities for trance called **"The Open Mind"** by Dawna Markova that is invaluable in understanding this concept in depth. One way to figure out what gets you into a trance state is exploring what stimulation really annoys you. Barking dogs, music you hate…creaking floors…auditory stimulation might get you into a deeper trance.

One of my jobs as a ritualist is to get a group into a trance state, otherwise known as an altered state of consciousness. Some people have an easier time getting into trance, others have more difficulty. Given that in a room of 50 people I'm working with every possible combination of learning modalities and intelligences, you can see where designing a ritual that is inclusive becomes a challenge.

Fire Pro-Tip: In a past article I discussed ritual disasters including fire. Fire is a fantastic way to involve all the learning modalities, but—know your fire. Practice with your flash paper, your flammable powder, your rubbing alcohol. Know what sets off that smoke alarm. Some of your attendees may be allergic to incense. One ritual facilitator told me about a ritual disaster: they wrote down intentions on post-it notes which they then tried to burn. What do post-it notes do? Stick to your fingers! Always test out your fire.

Multiple Approaches

With any of these techniques I'm offering the very briefest overview, and I recommend Googling to learn the basics of multiple intelligences. But here's a roughly of how you can design rituals to meet different needs working with my "polarities" model.

To make a broad generalization:
- Typically introverts are internal processors/long processors.
- Typically extroverts are external processors/fast processors.

In any group, there are folks that like to talk things out, vs. people who like to mull things internally. When you ask some people a question, external processors and fast processors typically have an answer right away with no problems speaking it out to the group, whereas other folks need a lot more time to process, and may be far less comfortable sharing with the larger group.

Sometimes shyness is a factor, sometimes not. It's not an issue of smartness, it's our brains processing information differently. In any ritual, I give the long-processors as much time as possible. If I'll be asking them questions in the ritual, "What do you release here in the Underworld," I'm going to ask the group to think about that question during my pre-ritual talk before the ritual. Ideally, I mention it in the email or Facebook announcement about the ritual so that people have plenty of time to ponder the question.

Opportunities for internal processing and external work:
- **Internal:** A trance journey where people have their eyes closed. I might have people do another internal activity like journaling or drawing out their experience.
- **External:** Have people speak to one other about their experience in the trance, or speak an affirmation to the whole group.

To make the external processing safer for the internal processors, and so it takes less time in a large group, I might break the group into a dyad or triad (twos and threes) to speak to each other. That's way less socially difficult than everyone speaking their intention to the whole group.

Audience Participation Pro-Tip: A powerful technique to work with more learning modalities and include people is to invite participation. However, ask the wrong question and you might be surprised how people participate. Or, you find that everyone is just staring at you because you didn't make it explicit that you wanted them to speak or move.

If people don't participate when I ask them to, I rephrase and repeat. "And now will you join me in speaking a word to call the air. Speak this word here and now, what would you ask of air? Will you speak it now? You, each of you, here in this circle, I ask of you, speak the words of the powers of air." All of that with deeper and more sustained eye contact will eventually get the group to participate. Having a few leaders who know to start speaking helps get the juices flowing.

Talky Talky Rituals
Many Pagan rituals are very talky. They are similar to the classroom setting where teachers present most information by talking. There's very little for kinesthetic learners. Are your rituals predominantly talky? How do you include your visual learners, your kinesthetic

learners, your emotional learners? How do you include your external processors?

In past articles I've talked about setting up altars and fire to engage visual folks, or engaging people in moving or doing some physical task in a ritual, and this is a big part of why. *Because it works.* Your own preferred presenting modality, statistically, is going to be auditory talking. But you have to recognize how many people this leaves behind.

There's the theory of the Golden Rule–do unto others as you would have done to you...however, when we assume that the experience of others is just like our own, we don't do a good job of designing rituals that are accessible to people different from ourselves. There's a saying in the field of web design and software usability, "You are not your user." You have to design a ritual that serves not just the way you prefer to do things, but how other people need it to be presented so that they can follow.

Boredom Pro-Tip: You have 2 minutes or less before people zone out on talky-talky pieces. Along with letting people know they can sit if they need to, you also have to basically shift gears and get people doing something every 2-5 minutes or you will lose their attention.

Chanting Pro-Tip: Singing a chant is a great way to get people involved. However, picking a complicated song for the group to sing does not build group harmony. Most folks won't know the words, and it does the opposite of a chant, it creates an energy disparity. Folks who really like that song are hyper and into it, and folks that don't know it, don't like it, or can't keep up...they don't feel like they belong.

Commitment

There are times when I choose to offer a ritual that's exclusive. If I'm facilitating a ritual that is an intense ordeal and includes fasting and physical hardship, that's not for everyone, and it's appropriate to offer that work if you make the expectations clear.

My commitment is to try and make accommodations where I can. Sometimes it's a matter of finances; I dream of the day when Pagan events bring in enough money so that I don't have to make the impossibly hard choice between an accessible and non-accessible venue, or so I can hire a sign language interpreter for a ritual.

Together there are lots of ways we can make our rituals more accessible and inclusive, and this is just the tip of the iceberg. Will you commit to inclusivity?

Note: Some content for this article was adapted from a post written by Shauna for the Pagan Activist blog: http://paganactivist.com/2013/07/21/ritual-physical-accessibility-transgender-inclusion-and-more/

Ritual Design & Facilitation: Chanting that Works

Published in CIRCLE Magazine Issue 115, Also published in Stepping Into Ourselves: An Anthology of Writing About Priestesses, Goddess Ink Press

"How do you get people singing?" people ask me. "How can I get my groups at home to actually join in the chanting voluntarily? I start singing the chant, and it stutters and dies horribly." I've been to the rituals where everyone mumbles along with the chant...actually, a decade ago that used to be me, secretly praying the chant would end soon.

Getting people to sing is extremely challenging, and I've been there singing a chant with people staring blankly back at me. Phaedra Bonewits put it succinctly in a sacred sound workshop she led at Chrysalis Moon festival, that once people developed the art of recording, now we don't hear a musician sing their "ok" version of the song, we only hear the best take out of multiple tries. Thus, we learn that we shouldn't sing unless we are perfect.

I am not a perfect singer. In grade school, I was the one the music teacher asked to sing more quietly because I was off key. When I started attending Reclaiming rituals, they encouraged me to sing anyways. Over time, I discovered that I could hit the right notes on the chants, I just had to sing them enough times to learn them. My voice got stronger.

Eventually, I began leading rituals on my own and there was no one to teach the chant but me. I survived, and learned how to do it better.

You don't need to be a musician to lead chants. Here are some of the tips and tricks that I've used. I haven't ever taken a music lesson, nor do I read music, though I have learned from some trained musicians like Lucinda Sohn, who's a former choir director. Primarily I'll use terms that you don't need to be a musician to understand.

Tone deaf
What people usually mean is they can hear that they are hitting the wrong notes, but can't make their voices sing the right ones. For most of these folks, the solution is pretty straightforward: sing more until you learn the song. Also, you might try singing the chant at a lower pitch; a lot of what I thought was me being tone deaf was just that I was trying to match my voice to notes too high for me to hit.

Learn the chants
I sang along to chants alone so nobody would hear me singing off key. I found that I needed to sing a lot of times to really learn a chant, to learn the correct notes through muscle memory. I can't teach a chant that I don't know.

Voice warm ups
Even after years of singing, my voice sounds terrible if I haven't warmed up. I need a half hour to an hour of singing to get my voice properly warmed up. I often sing in the car to get ready to facilitate a ritual. I'll keep singing until I can hit and sustain the higher notes in my vocal range. When working with a group, I try to find ways to help a group begin to warm their voices up such as toning.

The right pitch
You can't teach a chant at a pitch the group can't sing, and you can't lead a chant if it's too high pitched for your own voice. By pitch, I mean singing higher or lower. I don't know what key I am singing in,

but I do know when someone is singing a chant too high for my voice. If I'm leading that chant, I start it on a lower note so that I can sustain singing it.

I've found that inexperienced singers are generally more comfortable singing chants pitched a little lower. People not used to singing will drop completely out of a chant that is started too high. I've heard an axiom that you must start chants higher because they drop in pitch, but I've found is that chants drop in pitch because they are started too high. When I start a chant at a pitch most people can follow, the chant stays there.

Picking good chants
Perhaps obvious, but there are really a lot of bad chants. A good chant is simple enough that people can easily learn it, and musically complex enough to be engaging. This isn't easy to explain in text, but if you ever need some ideas for good chants, I'm happy to sing to you on Skype or into your phone, just email me.

Picking the right chant
Just because it's a good chant, doesn't mean it's the right chant. There are basically 2 kinds of chants; chants to hold space, and chants to build energy. There are energetic chants that would be hard to sustain for a long time, and there are droning chants that are impossible to build energy with. Generally, chants in a major key are easier to build energy with. Chants in a minor key are easier to use for holding space. Chants in 3/4 time (like a waltz) are easier to use for holding space; gently rocking, cradling. Chants in 4/4 time are easier for building energy.

Holding space in a ritual might be for an extended healing ritual, or to hear oracular messages from a drawn-down deity. A slow chant keeps the group energy focused.

An energy-building chant to build a cone of power works better with more complicated layers; two-part chants tend to build the energy more strongly, if you have a group that can sustain a 2-part chant.

Strengthen your voice and lung capacity
You may eventually want to take voice lessons. Singing while standing and projecting from the diaphragm will give you more vocal power. You can work over time to build up your lung capacity by singing tones like Om over and over. I can sing a chant for 40 seconds without breathing if I'm careful. Keep in mind singing notes at the higher end of your range take more breath. Having strong breath control allows you to keep singing as other voices tire.

Be loud, but not too loud
To lead chants, you need to project. You not only need people to be able to hear you, but you need to give the chant vocal power because your loud voice makes them comfortable singing. However, the trick is to sing with enough energy and enthusiasm to infect the group without overwhelming the group. Sometimes too much enthusiasm can turn the group off. You have to balance out your volume based on the group's energy level.

Honey, lemon, cough drops, and pickle juice
There are lots of remedies for helping soothe throats and removing phlegm. I spend an hour warming up my voice to get the roughness out of my voice, but Burts Bees honey and lemon cough drops have helped. Some like tea. Pickle juice can clear your throat out, but it's rough on your throat over time. However you do it, make sure your voice is clear when you start singing.

Advanced Skills

Permission to Suck
People get nervous when they are singing and the chant sounds bad, so I let them know that it's ok that it doesn't sound great at first, that we're learning the chant and it'll take 7-10 reps to just get the

melody. People feel less embarrassed and more willing to push through because I've given them permission to sound bad at first.

Off-kilter breathing

There are places where everyone breathes during a chant:

Oh, Mother (breathe) We are calling (breathe) Your children (breathe) we need healing (breathe)
Power, Power (breathe) Our love is our power (big breath)
(Chant by Alisa Starkweather)

With my lung capacity, I'm able to sing through the entire verse, and into the beginning of the next repetition, without needing to breathe. Why bother?

1. A big breath means a big silence. Singing through that adds vocal interest and maintains the energy. It helps to have multiple people trained to sing through the breathing parts, but one strong voice can do it.
2. When participants aren't sold on singing, they're waiting for any excuse to stop. When the chant leader takes a breath, what goes through their minds is, "Maybe we're stopping."

If I sing through when everyone's breathing, it never enters their minds that we might stop. This keeps the positive intention. I'm smiling and looking into their eyes while I'm singing, projecting the energy of, let's sing this because we can bring the deep magic.

Then I breathe after everyone has started singing the next line strongly. This is a difficult technique; I have to fight my body's urge to breathe when everyone else does, but it can be effective in getting people past the initial "hump" of the chant.

Smiling and charisma

I'm singing, not screaming it or frowning. I'm putting my life force and energy into the chant. I'm engaging people in direct eye contact, inviting them with all of my energy to join me. Here's how I find the energy to do this.

I go forward and backward in time; forward, to the moment when everyone is enjoying singing the chant and opening up to the divine. Backward, to the last time I sang a chant and the group connected to the magic. I'm using that energy to get people past the "hump." Your energy and positive intent is the fuel to engage the group.

Connecting with the group
Sometimes, you may need to start slower. I have seen some ritualists with hyper, over-the-top energy. The group recoils; it's too much, too fast, too showy. The trick is to meet the group where they're at, entice and engage them. Remember that amazing energy you want to evoke. If you fall in love with that moment, with that divine connection, where everyone is singing and connected and whole and holy, that is the fuel you want to bring into the chant you're singing. When I talk about authenticity in ritual, that's what I mean.

Developing other chant leaders
Helping others strengthen their voice and anchor chants will increase your ability to get a group of people singing; the more strong voices you have, the easier it is.

Harmonies
I learned to sing harmony by singing along with MP3's of chants and sang the wrong notes until it sounded right. Harmonies almost always add something, though you need the group to have a solid grasp on the chant before you bring in a harmony line. It's better if you have designated chant anchors for melody and harmony. If you can only add one harmony, go for a lower harmony; this adds a "floor" to the sound and it's vocally easier for most people to do. Someone with a higher voice can add a high harmony which pops up the energy.

Drumming

Drumming can either really add to the chanting, or completely collapse it. I've facilitated rituals where drummers with no rhythm joined in; once one of those drummers begins, it's pretty difficult discretely ask them to stop. An off-kilter rhythm can really throw your chanting out of whack. Typically I try to test out a chant with a drummer first or work with drummers I know, otherwise, I try to set up an agreement that drummers will drop out if I give them a hand sign. Skilled drummers can add depth to the space-holding chant and help an energy-raising chant build up.

Rhythm

People can snap, clap, and stomp if you model that kind of rhythm making. It may take a few tries before people join in. Let the energy of the group tell you when they are ready for rhythm. If you start clapping and nobody follows, they aren't ready and you can try again in a minute. Having other ritualists who will join in and model what you are doing encourages others to participate. Adding rhythm and other layers keeps the chant from losing energy when it hits a plateau.

Further Practice

There are more techniques, but hopefully these will be of help. The best thing you can do is practice and get better at chanting. Contact me with questions or topics you'd like to see addressed in future articles. Also, I'm happy to teach you chants over phone or Skype.

This article is published in Stepping Into Ourselves: An Anthology of Writing About Priestesses, which is an amazing resource for anyone involved in Pagan leadership and ritual facilitation. http://www.goddess-ink.com/priestessanthology.html

Additional Chanting Resources

First published in CIRCLE Magazine Issue 115

If you search on "Pagan chants" online, you'll find a number of chant archive websites in various states of abandonment. I set up a group on Facebook called Chants and Chanting where people can post what types of chants they are looking for, or post links to chants. It's been a useful group to find the authors of chants as well. https://www.facebook.com/groups/ChantsandChanting/

One of the consistent frustrations of people who want to lead chants is actually finding the melodies; most sites will just list the lyrics, and maybe an author if you're lucky. Occasionally some sites will have mp3 files of varying quality; sometimes the mp3 files are recordings of the professional musicians who composed the chant, but sometimes it's hard to learn a chant that way. Other times, it's someone singing the chant and with some frequency, it's not someone who has a great singing voice or they are having a hard time with the melody, so it's hard to learn a chant from that as well.

Thusly, here I'm posting a few of the chants that I use very commonly. I've put up an experimental version of my Intro to Chanting class on my YouTube Channel http://www.youtube.com/user/Shaunaaura/videos where I teach most of these chants. Eventually I plan to record mp3 files of each chant, as well as the potential harmony lines for the chants, so folks can download them and sing along to learn them.

Opening by Beverly Frederick
As best I know it's by Beverly Frederick; I've heard it used frequently in the Reclaiming tradition and hers is the only recording I could

find. I usually call this the Aaaa Ooooh chant, because it has two notes and two vowel sounds.

> *Aaaaaa, Oooooo,*
> *Oooooo, Aaaaaaa*

Other than having people sing "Om," this is about as simple as you can get and it's a great way to ease a group into chanting. Also a great chant to sing for a long time because it's simple. There's a second part to this song on Beverly Frederick's CD, which you can find on Amazon.com, however, I really don't use the second part.

Take Me Home Again by River Roberts
> *May my breath be a gift to you,*
> *Take me home again,*
> *May my _____ be a gift to you,*
> *Take me home again*

You can insert any one syllable word in there. Breath, bones, blood, heart, hands, voice, song, life...I tell people to pick a word, don't wait for me to pick one. The chant is in 3/4 time, so it's a waltz. River composed a second part to this chant, but again, I don't use the second part because I'm typically using this chant when I need something simple that the group can easily pick up.

Oh Mother by Alisa Starkweather
Note: I use the gender-neutral version, replacing "daughters" with "children." On Alisa's CD, which you can buy online, she uses the word daughters.

> *Oh Mother, We are calling, Your Children, We need healing,*
> *Power, power, Our love is our power*

The first line and the second line can be sung over each other to create more harmony and thusly to raise energy.

The Ocean Refuses no River
(comes from Sufi tradition, I've been unable to find an author)
Like Oh Mother, the first and second part (Ocean and Hallelujah) can be sung over each other to create harmonies.

> *The ocean refuses no river, no river,*
> *The ocean refuses no river, no river,*
> *Hallelujah, hallelujah, hallelujah,*
> *Hallelujah hallelujah, hallelujah*

Hold On by Starhawk
One part. Great chant for a new-to-chanting group. In fact, this is a chant that I can even sustain when I have a cold. It's available on one of the Reclaiming chant CDs. If you want to get fancy, you can sing it in an echo/round.

> *Hold on, hold on,*
> *Hold the vision, that's being born*

Ancient Mother by Robert Gass
The irony on this chant is, I typically use a gender-neutral adaptation so the words "Ancient Mother" aren't even used at all. You can find the original chant available on Amazon.com. How it usually goes is:

> *Ancient Mother, I hear you calling,*
> *Ancient Mother, I hear your song,*
> *Ancient Mother, I hear your laughter,*
> *Ancient Mother, I taste your tears*

My adaptation:
> *Oh Beloved, I hear you calling,*
> *Oh Beloved, I hear your song,*
> *Oh Beloved, I hear your laughter,*
> *Oh Beloved, I taste your tears*

Cracking Open By Lucinda Sohn and a bunch of folks at Diana's Grove

Cracking open, reaching down,
Rising up, I am growing

My adaptation, which takes language from Sufi tradition reflecting the idea that the heart must break to make more room for the light of the divine to enter:

Cracking open, reaching down,
Break my heart, let the light in

My Body is a Living Temple of Love by Robert Gass

Three-parter. Really potent energy-raiser if you have a large enough group and enough strong singers to do it.

My body is a living temple of love,
My body is the body of the Goddess,
Oh, Oh, Oh, I am that I am

Heart's Desire by T. Thorn Coyle and Sharon Knight

All one part. You can buy this one online via Thorn's site or on Sharon's Bandcamp page, lots of other great chants on that CD.

We dance in the heat of our heart's desire,
Dance in the heat of our heart's desire,
Open the gate, the key is within
To the temple of our hearts

Vault of Heaven by T. Thorn Coyle

Really worthwhile to buy the mp3 of this song to hear the layered harmonies on this 1-part chant. I have a second part I composed to add a high harmony for a particular ritual, and if there's interest I can sing it to you on Skype.

> *You who open the vault of heaven*
> *Out of the blackness come spinning of stars*

Sacred Fire (melody by River Roberts, lyrics by Shauna Aura Knight)

Another 2-parter. Drums are really helpful on this one to hold the beat.

> *Heart of the flame runs through my veins in this sacred fire,*
> *Heart of the flame runs through my veins in this sacred fire,*
> *We are holding a prayer for life force, Fire thank you, Fire thank you*
> *We are holding a prayer for life force, Fire thank you, Fire thank you*

Pour it Out for Me by Starhawk

This is the final line of a longer chant called Barge of Heaven. You can find it on the Reclaiming website on some of the older recorded Reclaiming chant CDs, but it's somewhat hard to hear how the chant is used for energy raising on that particular CD. The melody of this one-part chant is really potent and driving, but what makes it pop is bringing in drums, dancing, and high harmony.

> *Pour it out for me, pour it out for me,*
> *Everything you send me I will drink*

There's lots of other chants out there, and if you message me, I'm happy to point you to further resources. On my web site I'll be putting up chant teaching files as I record them, and links to good chant archives and places to buy CDs or MP3s of music by some of the great chant writers out there.

Section Two: Ritual Excellence

Ritual Design & Facilitation: The Shaman as Ritualist

First published in CIRCLE Magazine Issue 113

Learning to lead effective rituals is crucial—ritual is an essential service to our communities. Yet, I see a tremendous need in the Pagan community for a stronger commitment to excellence in the craft of learning to do this well.

Exploring the idea of the shaman is an excellent example of this. The words shaman, witch, druid, and priest/ess have many different connotations; I use these more as a job title than a description of a spiritual path. The word "shaman" was appropriated into English from indigenous Siberian tribes to refer to someone serving a community by fulfilling magical and religious functions and engaging in trance states and ecstatic rituals.

As clergy, leaders, ritualists, we serve our community. Whatever your path, you've inherited some of the traditional roles of the anthropologically-defined shaman. But shamans trained for years, decades. Even those in the modern world taking on the shamanic jobs of psychologists, therapists, and doctors, go through rigorous professional training. I believe that if we are fulfilling these roles in our community, then we must devote ourselves to the same rigor.

So how do we become better ritualists? How do we commit to excellence? What can the ecstatic trancework practices of shamanism teach us about effective ritual?

Excellence, Service, and Ritual
It can be difficult to learn anything beyond the theology of a tradition. I find that most people facilitate rituals the way they have seen others do them, which doesn't mean that they ever learned public speaking skills.

Those skills are different from learning elemental associations, the wheel of the year, liturgies, or about deities. While that's crucial knowledge to lead a ritual within your tradition, it's not the same as learning voice projection, body language, choosing and setting up a space that supports your ritual intention, or leading a chant and getting people singing.

Whether you lead a small coven or you lead large public rituals, if you've taken on serving your community through leading rituals, then part of that service must be committing to learning professional techniques to do that job well.

What is Good Ritual?
"Good" is subjective; rituals have vastly different intentions, and traditions can have completely different goals that rituals are supposed to achieve.

We can probably agree that bad ritual is clumsy, with speakers you can't hear. Reading an invocation off of a scrap of paper is not effective at engaging a group. It is absolutely appropriate as a learning tool when first starting out--public speaking is often our greatest fear. However, potent ritual comes when you understand the intention of each piece of your ritual, not just doing the pieces because that's what you were taught to do.

Intention

First, thoroughly understand the goals and intentions of your ritual: baby blessing, seasonal Sabbat, transformational ordeal, ordination? Go back to square one, even if you've led rituals for decades. What's the intention, what goals must it achieve? What emotional impression are you trying to evoke? What do you want participants to leave with?

Each piece of your ritual should support that intention. And each part of your ritual—grounding, circle casting, processionals, ally invocations—will have both a spiritual and a facilitation intention.

Example: Grounding/Centering

- **Spiritual intention:** To help people energetically connect to their deep selves and the divine.
- **Facilitation intention:** Help participants transition from the stress of driving to the ritual, to being present, let them know we're starting.
- **Facilitation techniques that won't achieve my goal**: A long meditation where people are standing, uncomfortable, and bored.
- **Better facilitation techniques:** A brief trance journey/meditation, some chanting, a drumbeat, or singing bowls.

Rule of thumb: People get bored in two minutes unless what you're doing is really interesting and participatory. Shamanic or ecstatic techniques utilizing embodied trance through chanting, layered sound, drumming, or movement typically more engaging for participants and usually take people deeper.

Missing the Intention

A common facilitation mistake I see is the boring logistic that takes forever, but it's The Way We've Always Done It ™. Most facilitation mistakes are honest ones, and come from well-intentioned folks who learned how to do ritual a certain way.

Example: Cakes and Ale

Often the intent is to help people to commune with the divine. However, a long, boring time span where plastic cups are passed out…one person slowly pours juice, another passes out cookies from a box…people get bored, they chitchat, they lose focus. The logistics have overrun the intention.

Solutions:

- Have multiple people handing things out, use a soft chant to keep focus,
- Completely remove those unsightly (and totally Earth-unfriendly) Styrofoam cups, while avoiding most food allergies/preferences, with platters of fruits and vegetables.
- Dispense with food completely and engage the group in chanting, dancing, and embodied energy raising for divine communion.

Rule of thumb: Ritual techniques that allow the whole group to participate and energetically engage simultaneously are more effective at engaging a deeper trance state.

Ecstatic Ritual

One of the primary reasons that I utilize ecstatic ritual techniques is that they help to engage participants in a deeper trance state or altered state of consciousness. Shamans have been using these ritual technologies for thousands of years, but they can be challenging for the modern Westerner to embrace. A great introduction to ecstatic techniques is the documentary Dances of Ecstasy, which you can find on Amazon.com.

Boiling these techniques down to their essence—we connect better to the deep, to the greater divine, when we are engaging our more primal mind. In "The Spiral Dance," Starhawk has called this engaging Younger Self to get to Deep Self; the goal is to get away from Talky Self.

Breathwork, music, chanting, dancing, drumming, all involve multiple sensorial input that engage the trance state. Using fire, layered colors, symbols, mythic language, or tactile experiences also work. An accessible overview of a range of techniques to engage trance states is Raven Kaldera's "Wightridden" which explores the eightfold path to altered states of consciousness.

Resources for Learning

It's hard to commit to excellence if you can't access places to learn. There are ways to get ritual training, but sometimes the cost of the classes and travel costs are beyond the means of many volunteer Pagan ritualists and leaders. However, sometimes it's worth the sacrifice of your time and your paycheck. Here are a variety of ways to explore gaining skills.

Ritual Arts Training

I learned most of my skills in the art of facilitating rituals through Diana's Grove and the Reclaiming tradition. Diana's Grove doesn't exist as it did. However a new organization, The Grove, is organized by River Higginbotham and other Grove alumni. They operate out of St. Louis, and I recommend joining their list to keep apprised of future facilitation trainings www.enterthegrove.com.

If you're interested in the Reclaiming Tradition, you might attend some WitchCamps. Often camps have specific ritual training classes, though you can learn just from experiencing their ecstatic rituals. Find out about WitchCamps and local communities at www.reclaiming.org.

Other ritual training that I'm aware of includes Cherry Hill Seminary (mostly online) and Ardantane (Albuquerque). Circle Sanctuary also has a clergy training program including ritual training.

Contact me if you are looking for local resources; those are too numerous to list here. For instance, in Kansas City, Gaia Community offers an Excellence in Ritual class for members based on techniques from Diana's Grove. I offer ritual training in Chicago and I also travel to teach, and I can refer you to other facilitators who travel to offer ritual training.

Pagan Spirit Gathering is a great way to get exposure to different styles of rituals, and there are workshops on ritual facilitation. Other Pagan conferences and festivals like PantheaCon, ConVocation, PaganiCon, and Pagan Unity Festival may have ritual classes too; you can check their programming online.

Broaden Your Horizons
Attend the rituals of local groups and travel to Pagan festivals and conferences to experience many types of rituals. You can learn a lot by watching what other ritual leaders do. The more rituals you attend from different perspectives, the more you'll learn. Observe what works for the participants, and what leaves them bored.

Public Speaking
Learning basic speaking skills is critical for ritual facilitators, yet it's one of our greatest fears. Find ways to take the pressure off and make it more comfortable to make mistakes while you're learning.

- **Joining Toastmasters:** This works well for some folks. Practicing public speaking when you don't have the pressure of leading a spiritual experience can help ease things.
- **Take a public speaking class, acting class, or improv comedy class:** Local organizations and community colleges will sometimes offer these.

- **Volunteer to speak:** Trying out public speaking for 2-5 minutes can help you build confidence. That can be at anything from your day job to the PTA, or you could partner with a local Pagan community leader who already does public speaking to get more practice.
- **YouTube:** While this isn't hands-on experience, search "public speaking" to find dozens of videos with tips.

Advanced Public Speaking

When you're confident enough, videotaping yourself will help get rid of Umms, You Know's, and seeing what your body language is communicating. Also ask people for feedback, though feedback from peers with facilitation experience usually gains more useful advice. Asking specific questions like, "Could you hear me even from the back" gives better information than, "Did you like it?"

Music

Music is one of the strongest ways to entrance and enchant a group, but if you're singing or drumming you need to learn to do it well. Strengthen your voice by singing chants; I sing for a half hour a day several times a week to keep my voice in shape. You might take a singing class or get voice lessons. Take a drumming class, or you can also learn other instruments like didgeridoo, shruti box, singing bowls, and gongs, all of which are accessible for non-musicians.

Brainstorm

Ask people what good ritual/bad ritual is; you'll find out a lot about how your rituals might need to adapt to serve your group. Ask people specific questions for feedback. Ask if the meditation was effective for them, or if the energy raising chant really engaged them.

Psychology and Educational Theory

Many of the methods that I have been trained in to engage trance states come from psychology, educational theory, and expressive arts theory. Take a psychology class, or read books on psychology; facilitating ritual is understanding people.

The most common educational theory tool I use is working with multiple learning modalities. Google searching brings up some useful articles. Basically, most rituals have too much talky-talky lecturing. This works for verbal learners but keeps us in Talky Self headspace vs. moving into deeper states of consciousness. Working with kinesthetic, visual, and nonverbal auditory techniques like chanting and drumming will help most to go deeper.

Lighting a fire engages most learning modalities—most Pagans light fires naturally, and it's a tremendously effective facilitation technique.

In general, any time the group has hands-on participatory experience vs. watching leaders do something engages them at a deeper level. It also helps to pulsate the types of experiences; trance journeys/meditations, or journaling, works better for internal processors. Dyads or declaring intentions to the whole group works better for external processors. Going back and forth engages both more deeply.

This newsletter has incredible articles: http://facilitatoru.com/blog/category/facilitation. They focus on meeting and workshop facilitation but the techniques are applicable to rituals.

Books
There are a number of books that offer ritual leadership skills, though I haven't found any that go in depth enough into facilitation techniques. Nevertheless, these two are an excellent place to begin: Isaac Bonewits "NeoPagan Rites," Amber K & Azrael Arynn K "Ritual Craft."

Also, if you are part of ADF tradition, Kirk Thomas of ADF has written some excellent online guides and articles for ritual leadership

Committing to Learning

If you are fulfilling the role of the shaman in your community, whatever the capacity, means you're committing to excellence. Future articles will focus on techniques to become a ritual professional including ways to get people chanting, setting up your space and using timeless language, and more ecstatic techniques in ritual to deepen the trance state.

Raising the Bar: Rituals That Pagans Look Forward To

I hear a lot of Pagans talk about rituals that are not engaging, and I hear from Pagans who stopped attending Pagan events because they didn't find any connection to the divine, or to community, through the public rituals they attended. And, I've attended my fair share of rituals that were not engaging at all.

I'm curious what others would like to see change with Pagan rituals. When I teach ritual classes I often begin by brainstorming. "What does bad ritual look like?" Think about that for a moment. What rituals engage your personal frustrations, whether the ritual is overly silly, overly serious, or just ho hum.

I would like to see a makeover of public rituals; or at least, of many of the public rituals that I've been to.

Basic Public Speaking Training
I think rituals can be lackluster because, in part, while we may get training in the ritual liturgy of a specific tradition, we're not necessarily trained in the professional skills needed of a ritualist. I've heard priest/esses invoking elements and deities with what was probably brilliant poetry, but either I couldn't hear their voices, or

they had no inflection in their voice because they were reading it off a piece of paper.

I've heard ritual facilitators ramble on for 10 minutes about a topic while the participants around me kind of chatted with their neighbors; he was droning on, and we couldn't really hear him anyways.

In the vein of seeking excellence in Paganism, I have seen some amazing rituals, and I really believe that dedicating to the craft of excellent public ritual is worthwhile for the whole community, so I'm writing this from a sincere place of love for community.

Some of My Biases
I find rituals that are just about doing ritual to be boring. I.e., "Oh, so it's Pagan Pride, I guess we should do a ritual." I tend to like rituals that have a deeper personal growth component. I also have a love/hate relationship with old time seasonal customs; I like the idea of them and the connection to the past, but many of those customs have no meaning or context for my urban ritual audience.

Or, they can bring up gender or other issues that are challenging in a modern context. One item some find offensive in ritual is the great rite represented by the chalice and the blade--that symbolism might work with a particular crowd that's keen on occult/alchemical symbolism, but for most of the Pagans with a feminist leaning, it's offensive. I don't really want to associate a penis with a blade.

I also have a bias toward ecstatic energy work, so I find that I enjoy a good chant, but many of the really bad Pagan chants out there that I've heard in rituals don't do anything for my spiritual experience. I love a musically interesting chant, preferably that doesn't have a predictable rhyming pattern, but that's simple enough for a group to learn.

For my part of the ritual excellence quest, I spent years learning how to be a professional ritualist at Diana's Grove, and then honed my skills after by offering community rituals, later traveling and teaching. I try to bring tools for ritual excellence to my community as well by teaching the ritual arts, and what makes a good ritual regardless of tradition.

It's possible to have a public ritual, that honors the season, and that is inclusive of the many folks present even if they are solitary and used to their own way of doing things, while also making space for people to go deep and have a transformative experience.

Ritual Focus and Intention
At Diana's Grove, the rituals didn't really honor the sabbats at all, though somehow I feel more connected to the earth and the cycles of the land doing rituals there. Diana's Grove rituals were based on the monthly intensives, and followed the arc of whatever myth or story was being used that year for the Mystery School. Reclaiming rituals typically honor the sabbats, but there's usually a focus on personal growth work as well.

If I'm offering a sabbat, I look at what's going on in the earth, and look at what's going on in the community, and I craft a ritual to give people personal work to do that is reflective of the season.

And it's true that if someone's attending one of my public rituals once or twice a year, they probably won't get to have as impactful an experience, because I believe that about half of a ritual's effectiveness is the ritual skills of the facilitator team, and about half is the involvement and investment of the community.

So if they don't know anyone and aren't really invested, then they probably aren't giving as much of themselves, and the way I see energy working, they don't get as much back either--I look like energy as blood flowing through a pumping heart. I have to give in order to get, or it just sits there and stagnates.

Emotional Connecting

It's hard to open up like that, and I can speak from my own experience. While I find that every Diana's Grove ritual I've been to has transformed me in some way, there were a lot of rituals I had a hard time allowing myself to emotionally connect. Maybe I had a bad day, or a disagreement with someone in community, or I had things on my mind and was frozen over.

I also have difficulties in general emotionally connecting to people. I also have a difficult time getting into a trance state, so there are a lot of times when many people in the group around me are deep in trance, and I'm kind of hanging out and metaprocessing things.

Facilitation and Connection

Having done so much facilitation work, I personally now find it's sometimes easier for me to have a trance experience when I'm facilitating the ritual; maybe facilitating keeps my conscious mind busy enough that my emotions can come out.
I also tend to have spiritual/divine communion experience when planning rituals; that moment of the shiver up the spine when I know the gods are there, part of the ritual, and that the working will work for the community. Often that's where I get my most profound experiences if I'm facilitating a ritual, before the rite for the group even happens.

Emotion and Better Ritual

The point is that getting a group of people to open up and feel is really the key, I have found, to creating more profound rituals, rituals that people enjoy and look forward to, rituals that actually give them the opportunity to connect to the divine.

I really feel compassion for folks who don't find they are getting anything out of public rituals. I think it's partly poor facilitation on the part of the ritual leaders, but, it's also that some of us just have a harder time opening up

I wonder how much of this comes from ritual form stagnation--where what many people were taught as the proper form for a ritual in their tradition, interferes with the ability to bring in or adapt ritual tools and techniques that would make the rituals more inclusive and engaging.

One-At-A-Time Logistics
To get into the nitty gritty of ritual facilitation, this is the biggest mistake I see people make as facilitators. Even little things like when people must line up at an altar to do something in the ritual, or when each person must smudge the person next to them in a circle. That can take a long time even with 13 people; with 80, insisting on the one-at-a-time form is excruciating.

At the same time, physically involving people in participating in a ritual is one of the most effective ways to actually engage participants, giving them buy in and a reason to emotionally connect.

It's just that it's usually one of the things that's the most poorly facilitated. One-at-a-time logistics like smudging and cakes and ale are a part of many traditions' rituals. But those, and other logistics, are often handled in a way that leaves the group bored instead of engaged.

Feedback on Rituals
I find it's a delicate balance to offer feedback on rituals. I'm not trying to insult someone's tradition and hard work. I'm talking about actual facilitation techniques and actual impact of ritual components on participants. Which ones work and which ones don't.

As I hear of more and more people who say they don't go to community rituals because they're bad, boring, silly, or in general just don't inspire them, it's really important to consider these things.

It's also worth pointing out that the ritual components that work on one group my not work on another. I work best with open-language trance journeys, rather than guided meditations which tell me exactly what I'm seeing, or with shamanic drumming which has no specific guidance other than the drum beating.

What Works?
I work best in an ecstatic tradition where there's lots of movement and opportunities to interact during the ritual, and where we close out with singing, dancing, chanting, and drumming, ideally with more post-ritual drumming too.

Some people really don't like active rituals like that. People are different. Things that work for one person won't work for another.

I've seen some people who really resonate with intensely scripted rituals and liturgies. Some people really resonate well with the really silly rituals, or with the really formal ones.

I find that I work well with rituals that are intense--where there's space for joy in our spirituality, but not likely anyone's casting the circle in a tutu with bubbles, unless it's a follies night with a talent show :D

Those of us leading rituals need to continue to raise the bar of excellence. We need to work to make rituals more impactful for our So--I wonder what leaders offering public rituals can do to raise the bar in ritual excellence, and to make rituals more impactful for participants, as well as more inclusive of different ritual styles, and more traditions than just Wiccan.

Ecstatic Ritual for Communities: Celebratory or Transformative?

Why do we do ritual? What is the purpose? Why is ritual so important to us? I have to say I'm in agreement with some things that mythologist Joseph Campbell referred to.

Ritual is important and it is often missing from our lives; I believe that rituals can help us with healing from things like break ups, keep us in touch with the seasons, and that in general, ritual is something that people do and must continue to do.

On the other hand, as one person put it on an email list, a lot of ancient rituals probably looked a lot more like a kegger than any formal ceremony, and many of our ancestors seemed to like to party.

I definitely agree that we need ritual. A lot of my work in offering public rituals to the Chicagoland community is to give people

(Pagans, alternative spirituality, spiritual but not religious) folks a chance to come together and celebrate.

Context Changes Things
However, I also do rituals in the city, and in the modern era, and that changes things a bit. I can say that, if I ran an eco-village/commune out in the country and we'd just harvested our first corn, we would absolutely be out there in the fields with a fire, probably some home brew, and a heck of a lot of corn put out there to roast, probably some singing, hooting, and hollering.

Intuitively, I think this is pretty much what our ancestors did for many of their seasonal celebrations.

Yet, here in modern America, the first strawberry of the spring is not a miracle. It's not the first fruit I've eaten since we started eating off our stores and supplies in November.
Actually, I can go to the grocery store and eat whatever I want at during any season.

When I do a ritual in Chicago, most folks have no context for what it was to be waiting and waiting and waiting for winter to break, so that we might get fresh food. The miracle of the seasons turning is not really a miracle any more. Sure, I get the winter blahs and spring coming back feels great, but it's not what my ancestors went through.

Transformative Ritual
Since there isn't the ambient energy of seasons turning being such a potent thing, and since people have far less connection to those seasons turning, I work to offer rituals that have a transformative component in them when I do public work.

I use the seasonal celebrations for theme, but I focus the ritual work on people and their processes. I do this to give people some kind of an anchor, something that will actually draw them into the season, as well as a shared context for ritual work together in a community.

People can't always get excited about Ostara and the first eggs, because they eat eggs all year long thanks to chickens raised with grow-lights. But they can certainly connect to, "What are the seeds you are planting?" People don't deeply feel the impact of Samhain, of that last harvest before we're shut in for the winter.

But they can connect to, "What is the harvest of your past year? What of this past year do you wish to hold onto to plant for spring next year, and what of the past year needs to die and become compost for the soil?"

Rites of Passage
I also think that more rites of passage in general need to be honored in a way that helps and heals. I think that weddings and funerals both get blown out of proportion and become these huge expensive things, whereas other rites of passage get short shrift.

Weddings--well, brides are expected to spend more than they have on their weddings and make a big deal about it, and I think this has gotten warped out of control. The expectations to do all these majorly expensive things is really ridiculous, and gets away from the basic spirit of the rite.

I say this, having orchestrated my own too-expensive wedding, even though I did organize a pretty cool costume masquerade ball very much on the cheap. I've participated in weddings that cost the bride and groom way too much and had them starting out their lives in debt, and I've stood up for friends who organized lovely meaningful ceremonies that didn't cost an arm and a leg and certainly were no less loving for it. Quite the contrary.

Funerals--well, here again, I have to say that the cost of a funeral is something ridiculous. If we were in a culture where a chieftain was buried with grave goods, that would be one thing. But if you weren't wealthy, your burial and funeral certainly wouldn't be something that would impoverish your surviving family. In February of 2011 my father died, and the cost of that was staggering. Even though we did not embalm him, we did not purchase a coffin, we just cremated him and had a short memorial service at the funeral home, and that cost about $5,000.

There's all these other rites of passage that we often miss as a culture, and I think people suffer for it. Pagan Spirit Gathering (PSG) offers some of these, which is really great. They do Croning and Saging rituals, as well as Young Men's and Young Women's rites of passage for our youth coming into adulthood.

Ritual for Community
Even the Transition Town movement that is focused on ecological sustainability suggests seasonal celebrations to bring the community together. These rituals are not about religion, they are about the season and community bonding.

I think that, whether you're based in the myths and traditions of a certain culture, or even if you're just looking to bring together a diverse community, ritual, gathering, and celebration is crucial. I think there's a place for both celebratory and transformative ritual, and it all depends on what's going on.

Ultimately, I think that the way I'm doing ritual more and more has nothing to do with Pagan, and everything to do with being human, being on an earth that turns and has seasons, being human in a community of other humans, and the way we gather changes over the course of those seasons.

More and more, I think ritual is just a way we are human together and help each other to be human, to celebrate our rites of passage, to honor our dead, to help each other get over the hurts and celebrate the joys.

Section Three: Elusive Authenticity

Urban Ecstatic Ritual

First published in CIRCLE Magazine, Issue 112

Facilitating rituals in a circle of trees with the glowing lights of ten thousand fireflies, or in the light of the moon next to a burbling creek, is different from gathering together in a rented room in the middle of a city. If you cannot do ritual in a forest grove, how do you still achieve the power of ritual in Nature? How can you get a group of urban Pagans into a state of communion with the divine, when the rumble of the train is passing by your venue, sirens and horns punctuate your rituals, and fluorescent lights glare down on your group?

Many modern Pagan rituals are about as non-ecstatic as you can get. Eighty people stand in a circle under the blaring sun, a couple of people stand in the center and read something off a script, it's hard to hear what they are saying over the buzz of the locusts, and then everyone waits while Styrofoam cups of juice laden with high fructose corn syrup and a dozen other unpronounceable chemicals and a plate of preservative-laden cookies are passed around.

If you've been to that ritual—or if you've led it—you know that just because a ritual is performed outside, doesn't mean that any communion with nature is actually achieved. And just because a ritual takes place in a hotel ballroom or a rented room doesn't mean that communion with nature or the divine is impossible.

The most powerful rituals that I have participated in and facilitated have used a combination of ecstatic ritual techniques, inclusivity, participation, trance work, and a focus on authenticity and deep presence. The question to ask is, what does "excellent" ritual look like, and how can we make our ritual excellent in any setting, given whatever constraints we are faced with?

What are the most powerful and moving rituals you have been a part of? What made them compelling?

There is a magic to some rituals that can be hard to explain, though some techniques can help you more consistently achieve that indefinable magic and communion when facilitating your own group or personal rituals.

Logistics Indoor and Outdoor ritual
There are benefits to rituals in either setting, things you can do in one but can't in another. Here are a few.

Outdoor ritual:
Pros: Magical ambience of trees, the scent of the land, opportunity for large fires, fireflies, moonlight, stars.
Cons: Bug bites, bugs landing in your mouth while you're trying to talk, bug sounds, loss of sound containment, heat and sunburn, potential for lack of privacy, difficulty in accessibility for folks with mobility challenges, potential for weather.

Indoor (urban) ritual:
Pros: Sound containment, privacy, control over environment with setup and not worrying about weather, less irritations like bugs, heat, sunburn, greater chance of accessibility for mobility challenged folks.

Cons: Less natural ambiance, glaring lighting, recycled air, sometimes can't use fire in ritual, Exit signs, mechanical sounds, creaking floorboards, city sounds like honking horns and trains, other glaring reminders of modern life.

In a nutshell, the advantages of most indoor rituals are that it's a lot easier to project your voice for speaking and chanting. Participants in the ritual are also more likely to open up and feel safe if they are in a safe space. Doing ritual in a city park could gain some of the magic of nature, but the risk of competing against the sound of a soccer game or wandering park-goers takes away quite a bit of the safety people need to truly open up ecstatically to the divine.

The advantage of most outdoor rituals is that there's simply a poetry in nature that no words, no mystery plays, can ever match. But how to get that kind of poetry, mystery and power, into any ritual, indoors or outdoors? How do you bring the magic?

> *"So do you have mighty bacchanals in her honor? ... Do you step naked into the sea-foam, chanting ecstatically to your nameless goddess while the waves lick at your legs, lapping your thighs like the tongues of a thousand leopards?"*
>
> *"You're making fun of me," she said. "We don't do any of that stuff you were saying."*
>
> --Neil Gaiman, *American Gods*

Ecstatic

What is ecstasy? The state of being ecstatic? The truth is that a lot of modern Pagan rituals have lost that ecstatic, transcendent, immanent connection to the divine. What I often hear is, "Well, that's another Pagan Pride ritual," or, "Yep, that's why I don't do public ritual, I get more divine communion doing the dishes at home and singing to myself." My own personal experience was that I got more out of drum jams and dancing at raves or clubs than I did at a public ritual. That was before I discovered ecstatic ritual through the Reclaiming tradition, and through Diana's Grove.

Ecstatic rituals use physical and trance techniques to help people more deeply embody the ritual work, to both go more deeply into the body and transcend the body simultaneously, which may sound like a bit of a paradox. Ecstatic techniques include getting people to sing and chant rhythmically, movement work, drumming, and other trance work.

While it is certainly possible to use ecstatic and embodiment techniques in a scripted ritual, actual ecstatic communion with the divine is far more difficult to achieve when ritual facilitators are trying to stick to a rigid script, whether that is a memorized script or one that's being read from.

Ecstatic ritual can also be hard to achieve when people are worried about looking stupid, and unfortunately, that is what modern ritualists have to contend with. In our modern culture, ecstasy is regulated in publicly-sanctioned doses. You're only supposed to dance and sing and cheer at a sporting event or concert. Only professional dancers should dance, only trained singers should sing. We're afraid of looking stupid in front of our peers, which is the basic psychological fear at the root of the fear of public speaking.

Similarly, I think many ritualists are afraid to ask people to take a risk, to step outside of their comfort zones. And let's face it, as a facilitator, you face a tremendous risk of your ritual failing if people decide to not engage in the activity you've planned.

Intimacy is a risk. Having an intimate, personal connection to the divine is a risk. Being witnessed by others in a state of pleasure or rapture, or in a state of anguish or grief, is a huge risk. A lot of our modern culture is structured around saving face, preventing embarrassment. Ecstasy and divine union through enjoying the sensations of nature, the sensations of dancing, the pleasure of singing across the circle and meeting eyes with someone, opens us to all kinds of potential embarrassment.

But what is the alternative? Ritual without feeling, without connection? So how do we take more of these risks in order to fully commune with the divine, and to help attendees at our rituals find that place of ecstasis?

Scripted Rituals
I have an admitted bias against scripted ritual, or at least, when the intention of the ritual is deep and cathartic actual mystic union with the divine. One reason is simple logistics of public speaking. If you listen, you will probably learn to tell the particular "sound" when someone is reading off of a script. Or even when they are reading off memorized lines. There is an unnatural cadence to the voice, and often a lack of emotional connection to the topic.

When someone has better public speaking abilities they can often mask this particular cadence. But even memorizing a script often still loses a great deal of emotional impact. People with a great deal of performance training, or some folks with a very natural charisma, can obviously get emotion and power from memorized words, but for most ritualists, it can be hard to have the time to memorize a script much less develop the kind of performance craft that will deliver that kind of power.

Another simple logistic is, if you're reading from a script that is in your hands, you've lost about half of your body language and the emotive power there. You've lost eye contact with your group, and your voice is naturally projecting downward into the paper instead of out to the group.

All those logistics combine to lose an incredible amount of the potency your words could have evoked in a group.

This isn't to say that if you're using scripts in rituals that you are a bad facilitator. Most Pagan groups out there are working with scripted rituals, and it's a very effective way to learn the structure of ritual. It's a great training technique to help new ritualists feel safe in taking their first ritual role if they only have a sentence or two to read off a piece of paper.

Scripted ritual can be a solid teaching tool, and there are some types of rituals that aren't overly adversely affected by a script.

But if your intention is helping people to feel the life force of the world around them, feel the divine pouring into their hearts, scripted ritual is going to have a difficult time effecting this unless you have a performance-trained ensemble ritual team.

Scripted rituals that are written by talented and poetic writers can also have a tendency to get overly focused on language that was inspiring to the writers, but that doesn't do much to help the group connect to the divine. Your words of divine inspiration may not be the words that get me to divine communion. In fact, sometimes all those words and all that poetry can get in the way. It just depends on the ritual, and the intention, and the group, and a number of other different factors.

Which isn't to say that rituals shouldn't be planned. What I'd offer is that rituals that have an intent to help participants ecstatically connect to the divine—these rituals are not written, they are designed. The phrase "writing a ritual" implies that the written form is the end goal. Designing or planning a ritual, however, implies that the end product is a moment in time, an experience, an event, that cannot be accurately captured on paper, which is how I see a ritual and how I work with the rituals I facilitate. A ritual isn't meant to be read, it's meant to be experienced.

It's worth working to find the balance of a ritual outline that has enough detail to provide guidance for everyone taking a ritual role, while leaving enough space for each person to find their personal connection and authentically bring that to the attendees and connect to the group.

Engaging the Group

What's left to you in a ritual that is designed to allow for participation and ecstatic connection to the divine, whether you are in the woods or in a rented room, is emotion, connection, dancing, chanting, and drumming. Music is a powerful technique, through chanting and drumming or other rhythm-making, to engage the senses of the whole group. Enchanting and engaging the group, though, is the most potent tool you have. By being engaged and enchanted by the topic, by helping people find their own personal authentic connection to the ritual, you will help any group to connect more deeply to the working of the ritual, connect to the divine, to each other, and to the deepest parts of themselves and their spirits.

By doing the deep work of learning first, as a facilitator, how to connect to the divine and to the energies you are working with, you open the way for your participants to be able to do that work. Subsequent articles on ritual will focus on tools to use authenticity, deep connection, inclusivity, presence, and charisma within ritual in order to increase the potency and effectiveness of rituals.

You may not have the twinkling of a thousand fireflies and a roaring fire under the stars, but what you do have is the magic you bring to the ritual. You have your voice, you have your eye contact, you have your own genuine connection to the work. If you believe it, if you are willing to go there first, if you are willing to feel deeply, you can begin to bring your ritual participants with you into the space of ecstatic connection.

Imagine we are all standing around the fire; it's indoors, so the fire is a low fire in a cauldron, alcohol burning on Epsom salts. We are singing. We come in closer. We have been dancing and chanting. We have journeyed and returned, we have laid down that which no longer serves us, and we have claimed the star-bright jewel of our destiny, of our dream. We are all reaching together. I am reaching for my dream, and I am reaching for your dream too. The chant begins to fade from words into tones, and our voices rise up together, we harmonize. We are looking across the fire at one another. There is a sweat-soaked silence as we huddle together around the fire, before we hear the roar of the train in the background, the siren in the distance.

Remember, we are nature too. And we, with our bodies and voices and our eyes, we can bring the wild, deep magic to any ritual.

Authenticity in Ritual

First published in CIRCLE Magazine Issue 113
(Co-Written by Steve Smith and Shauna Aura Knight)

To intentionally create impactful, meaningful ritual is a daunting task.

Steve notes that his early ritual leadership consisted of a good deal of unbound experimentation; they'd add whatever ingredients they'd read belonged in a ritual – a grounding here, an invocation there, and in the middle they'd insert something that looked like actual magical work – and just kind of hope it goes well. Shauna notes that her early years of ritual were just dancing into a state of ecstasis with no form or structure, and no intent to connect with anyone else.

Neither approach is effective at fulfilling the task of leading a group in connecting to the sacred, the divine, the larger Truth that we all seek in our own way. If we are to lead rituals that take us to the sacred depths, we must learn ways to bring the magic to our groups.

And yet, even when we learn public speaking skills and facilitation technique, why is it that some ritualists enjoy amazing success while others succeed only to a degree? Is charisma truly something that only some are born with?

The critical component in the alchemy of potent, compelling ritual is authenticity. It is the willingness to be witnessed in a state of communion with the divine. Not in a way that it's showing off, instead as a tool of service using your own authentic connection to help bring others to that place as well.

How to Bring Authenticity
Authenticity is the simplest thing in the world—oversimplified, it is when we genuinely feel something. But our culture trains us to mask it, bottle it into words and forms of expression that cause no discomfort. We're taught that revealing raw, naked, deep emotions is cause for shame.

You can't deny the emotive power of a proselytizing preacher on the sidewalk. He is shouting his truth, lit up by his faith and his connection to the divine. Then there is the wounded lover across the restaurant; her angry shouts carry truth and heartbreak. But either one of these is usually a call for us to look away, scorn them, to be embarrassed for them.

The feelings expressed, though, are real. They are humanity. They are the emotions we often long to utter, if we could. Authenticity is what stirs us. It's not being constantly explosive with passionate conviction, but it is believing in something. If you've ever loved, you've probably had your heart broken. If you've ever been inspired by something, you've felt yourself light up, get excited.

And in witnessing another's humanity, their real emotions, there is connection. There is an understanding of sameness, a kind of spiritual reunion. That connection is often uncomfortable, and resisted.

But in the ritual circle, where seekers come to open themselves to the sacred, that spiritual reunion is exactly what we are looking to achieve.

Having an emotional meltdown at every ritual is not the most constructive way to engage your group. Authenticity is much less about external expression than it is about being simultaneously fully present to internal, personal truth, while also being fully present to the ritual intention and to the group of people present.

Falling In Love
If you can imagine finding yourself suddenly deeply in love with a ritual experience, participating in a mystical exchange between yourself and the sacred space and all the participants in it...you may find that the walls of separation come down and the unfathomable beauty of the universe becomes clear in your mind for just a little while. And just like there's no one right way to express being in love, there's no one right way to express connection with the divine.

The goal of the authentic ritual facilitator is not to dictate the ideal form of expression, but rather to discover it – very often, to discover it in the middle of the ritual itself, from a place of intimately personal connection and trust.

Feel the Magic to Bring the Magic
The key to bringing authenticity and presence into a ritual is feeling and connecting. If you are going to bring that magic home to the group, you have to feel it first. How do you, personally, connect to the divine? How do you feel a deep connection to deities, elements, land spirits, kindreds, other spirits and allies? How do you know you are in the presence of the sacred?

Sometimes it's a sense of deep knowing that comes with a shiver up your spine; the hairs on the back of your neck stand up. Or maybe it brings tears to your eyes. Sometimes it is just a sense of correctness, of deep truth, in the words you are speaking or hearing. Sometimes it's a warmth in the belly, or the sensation of your heart chakra opening up. Sometimes authenticity comes with a shot of adrenaline or even a little nausea, depending on what you are connecting to and evoking.

But there very often is a strong embodied response, a physical or emotional reaction that lets you know you've hit the mark.

Finding the way that you connect to the magic is critical in bringing that to your group. If you are not speaking from a place of personal passion and genuine connection to the divine, it's hard to bring that connection to your group. When you have developed a relationship to the elements, you won't need to read up on those elements before facilitating an invocation. The invocation comes from your relationship to the elements, and the energy of the group.

Authenticity is in a lot of ways about being vulnerable, about being willing to share about your personal connection with a deity, spirit, or energy. When you bring that energy and life force of your own connection, you bring that spirit to life for the group.

Offering Connection
It is said that in a theatrical play, the audience is as much a part of the performance as the actors. In ritual, we seek to engage this on a deeper level, to make the audience into full participants. The participant must be able to take a piece of the magic with them when the ritual ends. Therefore, the nature of the relationship between facilitator and participant is different. Where an actor creates separation, a ritualist offers connection.

Connection cannot ever be forced; it can be invited, encouraged, requested, or offered. Connection requires willingness on both ends.

It would be convenient if we could assume that anybody who shows up to ritual is automatically willing to connect with us and with the rest of the group, but that's unrealistic, particularly in public rituals where the participants don't already know each other. Few people are eager to dive right into authentic connection with a room full of strangers. What we can assume of anybody attending a ritual of their own free will is that they're willing to work up to it.

So how do we offer them the chance to find their way?

The most important piece is to believe that each participant is a divine being and worthy of love and respect. And thusly, to make space to listening to the people at your ritual, to making space for them. This is core to leading from a place of authenticity, otherwise the authenticity you're trying to bring is just preaching or an emotional meltdown.

Listening

While there is some auditory listening in this, we're referring more to the ability to be energetically connected to the group. It's listening to the subtle emotional cues, being aware of your group's state of engagement with the ritual.

A ritual often begins with an energetically disconnected group; sometimes things are a little jumbled as people are on vastly different energetic pages. Once past the initial phases of ritual, in some traditions grounding and circle casting, in others a processional and opening meditation, attendees are likely already beginning, unconsciously, to express how engaged they are with the work through body language, eye contact, voice. Perceiving this state can be summarized as "crowd awareness."

Authenticity in ritual, then, is both the deep connection to your own inspiration, to the emotions that connect you to the divine, but also deep connection to the group you are serving in the role of ritual leader. It's being able to listen to where they are at, to be able to gauge how much intensity they are ready for, and when it's time to push the edge a little further to evoke deeper emotions.

Techniques to get to Authenticity

Opening to this place of connection can be more of a challenge for some than for others. You might begin with quiet meditation on particular elements, kindreds, deities, or other allies, or on other aspects of your spiritual work; the sabbats, the chakras, anything that is personally meaningful to you or that you want to learn more about. If quiet meditation doesn't work for you, try more physical meditations. Knitting, sewing, or painting while thinking can work well for some. Walking, running, or dancing might work for others.

If you're working to build connection with a particular energy, such as an element, writing things out can help. Shauna notes that when she was first taking elemental invocation roles, she'd write out a page or two of things that inspired her about the element and the theme of the ritual. Scripts or notes weren't allowed in Diana's Grove rituals, but she found that writing things out helped her at first, and eventually she didn't need to do it at all.

If you're seeking methods to connect to spirit energies at a deeper level, Diana Paxson's book "Trance-portation" is a great guide to deeper meditative journeywork. Patricia Monaghan's book "Meditation" offers a number of different meditative techniques if quiet/still meditation doesn't work for you.

Techniques to Connect to the Group
Several facilitation techniques are crucial for authenticity-driven rituals.

Eye Contact
The most effective way to convey your deep emotional connection to something you're working with in ritual is through deep, sustained eye contact. In our modern culture, eye contact is something of a shock. Deeply looking at someone while speaking about something that is impactful to you will get your genuine emotions across to that person.

Actually looking at people, coming up close to people and speaking to them in a conversational tone of voice, can break through some of those walls we hold up and allow participants to begin to follow you to that place where you're connecting to the deep and the sacred.

Inclusive Language
Language that seeks to invite vs. to tell. You are leaving out your own details and making space for your participants to have their own experience. Given all the work you've done to authentically connect to an element or deity, it might seem counterproductive. But ultimately, you're trying to find the common ground.

The trick is working from our personal experience and translating it to the universal. Invoking the experience of discovering a connection with the divine through an encounter with nature does not require us to spend fifteen minutes or more describing in painstaking detail everything we can remember of walking around the woods as a child.

What serves better is to remember the experience for yourself, let the feeling and sense of connection come back, and say, for instance, "Is there a place you have been, a memory you cherish, of being within nature and knowing that you are divine?" Be fully inspired in that moment by your own memory, and that inspiration, that authenticity, fuels the ritual participants to find the same.

Inclusive language in its simplest form is asking questions as opposed to telling people what something looks like. When you tell people something, you risk going into lecture mode, which puts people into audience mode. This is the antithesis of the kind of dynamic, energetic connection we are trying to establish.

Can you sense the difference between, "I see the Goddess, she is gowned in blue with long auburn hair, and I smell jasmine," and, "I feel Her, the Goddess...Can you feel Her too? Do you see Her? What does she look like? Is there a scent, or is there music?"

Instead of demanding participants visualize something specific, or engage in a particular movement, we can invite them to visualize what is potent and authentically inspiring for them. It's more potent to ask people what their place of power looks like than to give them the decorating run-down on our own. We're trying to use our authentic connection to help the group find their own, to make space or what inspires them and is most meaningful for them.

Because, when the group "buys in" to what's going on in the ritual, that's when the magic really starts to happen.

Authenticity in Ritual: Going Deeper

First published in CIRCLE Magazine Issue 114
(Co-Written by Steve Smith and Shauna Aura Knight)

There's an excruciating intimacy to letting someone in on your own personal experiences, to having your naked emotions witnessed...and this is the power that drives some of the most potent rituals. As a facilitator, that means holding incredible discernment between diving into "too much information" and yet going deep enough into personal vulnerability that serves the group.

Many Pagan rituals feel unsatisfying when the design of the ritual doesn't support the intention. An example is a ritual where the facilitators want the attendees to get into a deep communion with the gods, but the ritual they've designed better supports a lighthearted celebration of the season. There are many intentions for rituals, but the structure of the ritual and the techniques employed must support the work.

If your intention is to take people into the depths, one impactful technique is being willing to go into the dark places first, to speak the truth of your own story.

The greatest thing we ask of our participants is their trust. Trust is crucial to our goal of bringing people into a state of ecstasis, of connection, of communion. Imagine what happens when you observe someone who is faking something. How much are you willing to trust them?

In order for our participants to get the most out of ritual, we require trust given freely – and authenticity is the only coin with which to earn it. Participants can tell on some level when they are being fed something false.

Our job is to create and preserve a safe, sacred space full of invitation so that each participant makes choices on their own terms. We offer participants the opportunity to have experiences they would normally not be able to have. We offer safety, community, and intimacy. We offer risk and challenge and choice, we offer honor and sacredness to each person. Thus we serve as leaders, teachers, and ritualists.

How Does it Work?
At a Samhain ritual that Shauna facilitated, she could sense that the group was afraid to get too intimate, too real. Part of the ritual intention was connecting to ancestors and facing shadows, and the group was finding ways to distract themselves from the intimacy of the moment by making jokes. Laughter often masks nervous tension.

Once the laughter died down, she spoke about her father who had passed away, about what his message to her from the Underworld was. Her tears and sharing cracked open the group. They began telling their stories. Their tears spilled forth. To bring participants to the place of catharsis, we must be willing to go first.

Telling a personal story is one way to connect authentically to what inspires us, and to bridge that connection to the group. The challenge is making that story specific enough to be evocative, and open enough to be inclusive. In our Authenticity article in last month's issue we discussed inclusive language. Taking that further, it isn't our job as ritualists to tell people what their experience should be. It's our job to make room for others to experience things for themselves.

Can you remember a moment when you knew you were connected to the divine?

Perhaps your immediate response is "Yes!" Perhaps you find yourself in some doubt. "Is my experience similar to everybody else's? Does it qualify? What if my answer is no – does that mean I can't be authentic?" This is normal. There's a lot of pressure around that question, especially for those of us in spiritual service.

The divine has many forms, and comes to each of us in different ways, sometimes dramatic and other times simple. We can describe to each other our own experiences of the divine, but they may not always make sense to someone else. We know our experience because it's what we've lived and experienced, not because of what a person or book told us.

When articulating these experiences, sometimes it can be useful to omit specifics and focus on what is universal. Going on about a particular obscure deity might not really do much to include the group. Instead, we're trying to communicate that sense of connection. The specific for me might be the golden-bright sensation of the universe's breaking heart dripping like honey over my skin. It might be sitting at a café talking to Hades. It doesn't matter if our experiences of the divine look alike; they still connect us.

Many of us have faced spiritual crisis. Steve notes that when he faces the ongoing darkness of loss of faith, the pieces at his core that bring him back from despair are made from the experiences of connection to the divine. If Steve speaks in ritual of the dark nights of the soul he has faced, participants will resonate, and think of the times they too have passed through shadow.

Each of us has memories that impact us deeply. Building on the memory of your personal experiences, consider the ways in which those experiences have guided you on your journey, and how those powerful experiences might help others. A time you overcame a challenge. A time you felt beaten down by life. A time you helped someone. A time you harmed someone. A time you fell in love, a time your heart was broken. We are leaders, and we are human. It is our mistakes and fears that make us wounded healers who can help those we serve.

The Truth About Charisma
People often envy the charismatic. Charisma in ritual is being inspired by the larger vision, the divine, genuine emotions…and being able to connect that feeling to your participants.

Authenticity can be soul shattering work. It's not about putting on a show and being the star—it's about being willing to be seen to the depths, sharing the emotions that are difficult to reveal or hard to put into words. It's engaging people, enchanting them by the beauty of speaking truth from your heart. It's cracking open your own heart for the group you serve.

Somehow, even when we've had a bad day, we facilitators have to find the energy within ourselves to motivate the group. The facilitator puts out energy at the beginning of a ritual to help the group be willing to go deeper. The group responds to the authenticity and that's when the magic of charisma pays off. As the group goes deeper into their emotional connection, that energy builds and in turn can inspire the facilitators; it pulsates back and forth.

What gets a group to a place of depth is genuine emotions. And for a facilitator, that means a lot of personal spiritual work and a lot of personal risk.

You can learn facilitation techniques, public speaking, chanting, but there's no substitute for confronting your shadows, your fears, your deepest emotions. There is where much of your power resides.

That kind of intimacy can be terrifying at first. To actually share something personal. To perhaps be willing to be brought to tears in front of your group, to be moved to joy or anger, to be witnessed while feeling. To speak excitedly about something that inspires you, and take the risk that others will not respect you for your passion. It requires deep work not just in connecting to the elements, deities, and spirits, but also to understand our own issues.

Techniques:

- **Buddy up:** If you're having trouble emotionally connecting in ritual, a potent tool is to partner up with someone who has an easier time going emotionally deep. Looking into their eyes; their intensity and emotional response can call up an answering response in you.

- **Participation and Inclusion:** Getting participants to join in adds more life force, and vitality to your rituals. Turning attendees from audience members who are observing into active participants opens them to the energies of the ritual, which in turn, helps them connect to the deep magic. Share your own story, but invite them to participate.

- **Authenticity Exercises:** If you have the benefit of working with others, a technique that Steve and Shauna learned through Diana's Grove and Reclaiming is having several people standing back-to-back with eyes closed in groups of two to four. Each one picks a particular element, deity, or other spirit ally to work with. They are guided in a trance journey to help them connect to the ally or energy. The people standing speak (simultaneously/overlapping) whatever words come to them, even if it's just "Fire, fire, fire." The overlapping voices pull each person into a deeper trance state. Not being the only speaker, and speaking with eyes closed eases their nervousness. Eventually, this practice should begin to transition to speaking like that with your eyes open, and then, speaking alone vs. back to back.

Authenticity Vs. Scripted
Generally speaking, scripted rituals make authenticity more difficult. Most people stumble over half-memorized lines, never achieving emotional connection. Just because the writer was divinely inspired doesn't mean that speaking those words will inspire the same emotion. If you have performance experience, or if you wrote the ritual, perhaps you can pull it off. However, just getting volunteers to memorize lines is tricky. If you're reading lines someone else wrote, it's unlikely that those words will feel at home in your own mouth. It's not impossible to achieve communion with the divine with a scripted ritual, it's just unlikely.

Reading from scripts in hand removes most of the evocative power of your words and negates most of your body language. There's rarely room to adapt a script based upon the needs of the group or things that come up in the midst of a ritual. Shauna's article "Urban Ecstatic Ritual" in issue 112 goes into some additional challenges of scripted ritual.

Performance skills
Basic public speaking skills, staging, theatrics, lighting, and more are a part of ritual work. There are a number of performance skills, though, that can be over-used in ritual. One common mistake is an overly-loud, over-the-top voice. While this voice can be effective during some rituals, if that's the only ritual voice you're ever using, it's probably too bold and brassy and won't serve to help the group connect. If you've watched a big performance piece in the ritual and felt like it was too showy, then it probably was.

An easy exception could be if you are calling a god of thunder, or calling the terrible and lovely depths of the ocean and you want big sound and a feeling of vastness and majesty.

Most often in ritual, though, we're working to connect individually to each person. Think about the tone of voice you might use to tell a friend you care about them, to tell someone you love them. You probably aren't going to use big theatrical gestures and a big over-articulated voice.

The trick is to speak as you normally would, but loud enough that they can hear you across the circle.

The simple thing, genuinely spoken, almost always has more power than the big showy thing. In the PSG Women's Ritual in 2011, each woman spoke something genuine to each other person in the ritual. Each woman said, "I love you, I believe in you, I support you." Hearing this and speaking it sent most women into tears. Most of the people there had no public speaking or performance training, and they didn't need to memorize a script, they just said something genuine. This created an intensely emotional experience.

There are times in rituals where performance skills and theatrics can have a positive impact, and other times it's too brassy.

Deep Work
Authenticity requires brutal self examination; it's a personal risk for a ritualist. People might laugh at you. They might not like what you have to say. But in the end, committing to authenticity as a practice not only leads us as ritual facilitators to be better people with a stronger connection to the divine, it also leads to rituals that offer intimate and deeply impactful experiences for participants.

Ultimately the value of a many Pagan spiritual practices is the cultivation of a personal divine connection. Perhaps the next time you find yourself facilitating a ritual, you'll remember your own experiences of the sacred, or even just the really impactful emotional moments of your life. And you'll remember that all around you are those who are seeking an experience of their own.

Perhaps you'll take a moment to breathe in and become aware of the awesome honor and privilege afforded to you by them. Finally, maybe you'll understand a little more deeply that what they need – and deserve – is enough of your respect to be not only skillful, but also true to what you love, so that they might decide for themselves to share that connection for a moment.

And if you do, then for that moment, you will very surely be a servant of the divine.

SHAUNA AURA KNIGHT

Deepening Relationship with Deity Through Artwork

First Published in a Chicago Reclaiming newsletter

It's getting crowded in my art studio. Brigid, the Horned One, and a Moon Goddess all stare down at me from my walls. It's occasionally a little intimidating.

Though, I did invite them all here...

How did this motley crew of deities assemble in my painting studio? The answer is that, over the past months, I have been painting 4 x 8 foot panels of deities and archetypes. What I have found is that creating these paintings is a great way to establish a relationship with a particular deity or archetype. Whether you are preparing to work with a deity in a ritual, or preparing to aspect or draw down a deity, doing some kind of artistic work with an archetype, deity, or other spirit can help you connect to their energy.

What is Deity? What's an Archetype?
I should do a little "definition of terms" here before we go any

further. Many Pagans have differing belief on what deity is. Is Brigid a deity, an entity, an actual independent consciousness? Or is she an archetype representing certain facets of the collective unconscious, or even, just a part of my own consciousness that is what the Brigid archetype represents?

I can really only speak to my own theological beliefs. It's up to each of us to determine where we are theologically and cosmologically—I'm certainly not here to tell you what to believe. I can only share with you how I work with deities and archetypes, and in specific, how this particular technique of making devotional art has helped me to connect to those energies and spirits.

I tend to be more of a pantheistic or archetypal Pagan, vs. a hard polytheist. Most days I work with the idea of a larger Divine/Mystery, and that any deity I work with is a piece...a story...an archetype...that smaller piece helps me to grasp the larger Whole.

Whether or not you believe deities are freestanding entities, or just methods of accessing the greater Mystery by working with that archetype, you can learn a lot about them by opening your mind to a conversation with them.

The Conversation
The first of the large-format paintings that I completed was intended as a deepening dedication to a goddess of moonlight and waters. I have worked with her for many years, though she isn't specifically a deity from any one pantheon. As I painted her, I did what I've often done while painting or writing fiction. I began a running dialogue with her in my mind.

The painting was intended as an invocation, a dedication, a devotion. But in structure, it became a conversation. I spoke to her, and I heard whispers back. Next time, I painted the Horned One, and the conversation became a little deeper.

Before I go further, I should define a few more specifics, because I know that when I first heard about people "talking" to Gods I was pretty skeptical. Or, I thought, "Maybe I'm not doing it right because I don't actually hear them or see them."

All of these conversations are happening in my mind. And the logical/conscious part of my mind insists that I'm just talking to myself. The more open-minded/younger self or deeper self part of my mind insists that I should just open myself to the possibility of the divine talking to me.

And in the end, I sit the fence, much as I do with the "what is deity" question. I accept that, whether these conversations and intuitions are coming from a deeper place inside myself, or whether they are coming from outside, from a deity, it doesn't really matter. The point is that this is an exercise you can use to reach these deep places of insight. So, I let myself question my sanity, laugh, and keep going with the painting.

How Does This Exercise Work?
Much like with any ritual work, opening myself to Mystery seems to work best when I move beyond the conscious/rational part of my brain. Starhawk, in "The Spiral Dance," talks about using ritual tools to engage Younger Self, who thus has access to Deeper self.

My best guess is that by keeping our creative brain in charge by doing something very artistic, while focusing on a chosen archetype, each of us can become more open to the conversation. Which may be with words, and may just be images or feelings. I found that if I could suspend my disbelief a little, I would learn things I didn't know before, or deepen my knowledge of things I thought I already understood.

For me, the most intense experiences have been when I am painting the deity and their eyes are open, staring at me. However, I have done this exercise while making mosaic objects for each Element, and I still found it led me to insight.

If painting's not your thing, sculpture, music, dance, collage, poetry, creating devotional jewelry, or other art-making could be used to build this relationship.

The Horned One so far has been the most intense experience. I painted him because I was supposed to invoke him in ritual, and I'd never invoked a deity before in a ritual (except as a solitary). Also, I didn't feel I knew a lot about the Horned One.

My basic process was to first read up on the Horned One. There came a point in my research where I really felt the need to just start painting; I usually do a lot more sketching first, but this time, I dove right in. The conversation soon developed, getting more specific with each coat of paint. Initially the conversation was about musculature and pose, but it expanded to discuss the archetype and his mysteries. And whenever "rational brain" tried to check-in, I'd gently set it aside and get back to my painting.

Trying This at Home
When you're doing deep work like this, I've found it makes sense to do it in some form of sacred space, or at least, ensuring that you won't be disturbed. For me, doing any deeply creative work inherently puts me into what I'd call "Sacred space mindset."

It's best to paint when no one else is around. The conversation gets deeper when you don't have to respond to questions about dinner from your spouse. I usually play a soundtrack of music appropriate to whatever deity I'm working with, as that also helps me stay in the right mode.

Realize that when you do a deep invocation like this, you are building a strong relationship. Before you choose to do an exercise like this, do your research. Know what that archetype is about, and what it will ask of you. I had not deeply worked with the Horned One or Brigid before, but doing the paintings took my work with them to a far deeper level.

What Results From this Exercise?
Each of the paintings led me to a deeper understanding of the deity, the archetype. They each helped me to build a relationship with that deity. When I stepped into the circle to invoke the Horned One, he was no longer this colossal thing I didn't understand and was afraid of. He was this piece of Mystery who'd been talking to me for weeks. I didn't panic about the laundry list of things I had thought I would.

Instead, I felt like I was reaching out a hand to a friend that I knew.

Whether I believe I was talking to a deity, or I believe I was talking to an archetype inside of my own head, each is valid. This work helps with getting to know the elements, the Major Arcana of Tarot, or a deity prior to aspecting. Before I draw a deity down into myself, I want to know them outside of myself, and I want to be comfortable talking to them.

If painting isn't your thing, there are ways to do this through sculpture, collage, or other methods. Mosaic, devotional beads/rosaries, poetry…if there's a creative aspect, there's a way to use this to connect to the deities, archetypes, and spirits.

Section Four: Using Myth and Story to Craft Rituals

In the Forge Fires: Transformative Ritual

First published in Global Goddess Oracle Imbolc 2013 issue

When I facilitate public rituals, they are usually either connected to one of the sabbats, or seasonally-inspired at a festival or Pagan conference. However, the focus of the rituals is more on personal transformation than on seasonal celebration. My calling, as a ritualist and as a spiritual seeker, is to help people connect to the greater divine within and without, and to help people transform into the self that they wish to become, the self that can change the world.

So many people I know are held back by old wounds, old stories of powerlessness. I know people of all genders who feel like their lives are stuck. They are not living a life of meaning, and they dare not reach for their dreams.

There's a particular ritual pattern that I often use near Imbolc. I work in an ecstatic, extemporaneous ritual style similar to Reclaiming, so rituals aren't scripted so much as designed in a particular flow and then co-facilitated by a large group of facilitators. Thus, any time I've done this ritual it turns out completely different based upon who is there, and the group that attends. I've found this basic ritual outline to be a useful pattern to help participants engage in an accessible process of personal transformation, and to experientially work with the idea that we each are a part of a larger community and tribe and how our own personal work and gifts impacts the communities we engage in.

It's also a great ritual to help new ritualists step into more significant ritual roles that aren't too overwhelming.

I learned ritual facilitation from Reclaiming and from Diana's Grove; Reclaiming's ritual format is informed by the Feri tradition, and by what I'd call post-Gardnerian Wicca. Diana's Grove adds further influences from Jungian psychology, educational theory, and a strong focus on personal work via Jean Houston's Mystery School. The ritual format I use makes an assumption of a circle casting, elemental invocations, and deity invocations, though certainly this ritual could be adapted into a different tradition that has a different ritual structure.

I should also mention that the words I'm using in the outline below for pieces like the elemental invitations are just seeds of an idea; in an ecstatic ritual, each person would take one of these ritual roles and spend 1-2 minutes not only talking/building the theme or idea, but also engaging the entire group in an activity to connect to that element or ally through some participatory action like speaking, moving, or singing. The ritualists taking on the various Brigid roles would have spent time learning about and working with Brigid.

1. **Pre-ritual talk/workshop:** I spend 15 minutes or so talking about ritual theme and working, teaching the chants,

and covering any logistics so nobody's confused once the ritual starts.

2. **Gathering:** A process I learned at Diana's Grove, we begin with singing, chanting, movement, to build energy and begin the process of connecting as a group. This is a powerful tool to begin to engage a trance state.
3. **Grounding:** A brief meditation to connect to our bodies, to the space, to the season (Imbolc), to the personal transformation we are doing, to spiritual/divine energies.
4. **Circle Casting:** Engaging the whole group in some activity to connect together, to quicken and crystallize as a group, not just as a bunch of people who showed up for a ritual. This could be the circle as the seasonal wheel of the year, or it could be having everyone speak our names to engage ourselves as co-creators of this circle.
5. **Elemental Invocations/Invitations**: These should begin to invoke the altars/points on the journey we'll be working with later in the ritual.

    a. **Air:** The fire of creativity, the fire in the head and heart, together we blow the breath of inspiration to kindle the fire we hold cupped in our hands, the fire of our gifts that we bring to the world
    b. **Fire:** The forge fire, the transformative fire, the fire that blazes hotter than all the metals. When we stand in this fire, all that holds us back and does not serve burns away.
    c. **Water:** The sacred well. The depth of dream and the unmanifest potential. When we dip our hands into the sacred well waters, we find our own gifts, our dream, the starstuff we are made of.
    d. **Earth:** The hearth fire, the healing fire. The fire that we each tend. When we've blown the kindling to start the fire, how do we keep it going? How do we care for each other, heal each other?

e. **Center/Spirit:** The place where all the elements come together, the center of the world. Alternatively, the world tree, the axis mundi bridging the worlds, or this could be the communal fire, the center of the tribe, the fire of community that we gather around.

6. **Deity/Ally Invocations**
   a. Ancestors and Descendants, Fae, or other kindreds if you honor them
   b. Brigid/Bride/Brigantia. However many people are anchoring the Brigid altars (below), each of these should speak at least a few words about the facet of Brigid they are representing.

7. **Storytelling/Trance Journey:** One to three facilitators begin to tell the story of the season. Encourage participants to get comfortable, sit or lie down as the storytelling turns more into a Trance Journey. I use the "dual voice" technique where two or three voices are layering over one another. We tell the story of Brigid, of Imbolc, of what it is to be safe and warm in the depths of winter by the hearth fire. That the hearth fire that protects and warms us comes from wood. That wood has been gathered by someone, and the fuel is running out.

   We must go out into the woods on a journey to collect the fuel to bring back to this fire that warms our tribe. The journey establishes that we each have a personal magic, we each bring unique gifts to the world, and that the divine is reaching for us, encouraging us to use our gifts and to reach to bring our dreams into reality.

8. **Journey to the Altars:** The trance journey transitions by asking people to stand, to journey the various Brigid altars. This can be done where people visit each altar asynchronously (the order doesn't matter) or with a linear

progression (Sacred Well, then Creative Fire, etc.) This depends upon the size of the group and the ritual intention; standing in line gets boring and can take people out of ritual headspace, though I often use a chant to hold the space. I'll go under the assumption of a linear progression.

One or more people aspecting/oracling/drawing down Brigid anchor each altar, speaking in a trance voice—in other words, low voice, with slow, even pacing—to ask questions of each participant. The altar could be a small decorated table; it could be a room in a multi-room venue with theme colored drapes and candles, or it could be in a bower of trees along a path.

a. **Sacred Well:** What gifts does the sacred well hold for you? What lies within the dreaming for you? What is your personal magic? (Multiple people anchoring this altar means, the questions could overlayer and overlap, which engages a deeper trance experience for participants.) Typically I use a large bowl or bowls with blue glass stones or beads and participants choose one.

b. **Creative Fire:** You hold your gift in your hand. Breathe your life force into it, quicken it, kindle it. This is where the water of the divine fills you to become the fire in the head and in your heart. What is your creative inspiration? What is the name of your gift? What magic do you bring to the world?

c. **Hearth Fire:** Holding gifts from the divine, holding magic—these, like fire, must be tended. How do you tend this fire? How do you grow it? How do you learn to use your gift, how do you grow your skills? How do you build up the fire?

d. **Forge Fire:** You have pulled this gift from the sacred waters of creation. You have breathed your life into it, tended it. And now, I ask you to give it up. To throw this piece of your own personal magic into the fires. It is such a risk to do this, but will you risk it that you might become more than you are? Will you burn away all that does not serve you in order to burn the brighter? What falls away? What old stories, what limits, do you release? (If I have access to an anvil or an approximation, Forge Brigid is hammering, and asks them to surrender their magic stone, which she "hammers" to produce a new stone, perhaps of a different color.)

9. **Return to the Center/Energy building:** When people have processed through the altars, I have them return to the center, or the bonfire, so I know when everyone's done. If people have been singing a chant to hold space, I let the chanting fall to silence. Depending on the intention of the ritual, the Brigids might address what it is to have these gifts.

I have each person put their gift into a bowl near the fire to actualize adding their fuel/gifts to build the communal fire while they speak aloud what their gifts are that they are offering to the community. Other things I might have people speak aloud to be witnessed are, what are the dreams they want to manifest, what the fire is they wish to kindle within themselves. In a large group this is people speaking out simultaneously, in a small group it's going around the circle in turn.

We transition from that into an energy-raising chant. In the rituals I work with, the energy raising is the "juice" that fuels the transformation we are asking for—the burning away of the stories that no longer serve, asking for Brigid to bring fire and energy to us that we may use these gifts, etc. This is also using ecstatic chanting, dancing, and drumming to move into ecstasis where it can be easier for us each to connect to the divine in our own way. The energy builds into a peak, and then falls. Usually I have the Brigids offer a benediction and blessing after this.

10. **Devocations/thank you's:** Thanking allies we invited into the circle and opening the circle.
11. **Community social time, potluck, drumming, dancing:** After a community-building ritual, having time for people to connect and talk is good for building a group with more long-term sustainability.

Ritual Goals and Intentions

This is a great ritual to facilitate healing work within a community, or to inspire community members to become more involved, as well as to offer a path of personal transformation by empowering people to not only identify and honor one another's gifts, but also to leave behind disempowering stories.

This ritual also works as a useful method of empowering new ritualists to take roles. As a feminist, I highly value sharing skills so others can learn to facilitate rituals, and learn solid public speaking techniques. One reason I teach ritual arts is to help people learn to make good rituals happen for themselves instead of waiting for people in power to do it for them. Encouraging new people to take ritual roles engages them in the community. Teaching good public speaking skills empowers them to do it well.

Public Speaking and Bringing Our Magic

The truth is, any one of us can be charismatic if we have learned basic public speaking, and if we speak truthfully from the heart. Each one of the Brigid altars could be anchored by one or three people, depending upon group size. Newer ritualists feel more comfortable doing work in pairs or small groups, though a single person anchoring an altar is not too daunting. The focus in this ritual is at most a light aspect of Brigid vs. a full trance possession.

The elemental invocations can be done by one or more people; they could be done by the Brigids, or they could be done by other folks. This is a ritual that could be put on by five people, or by thirty, depending on how many people you are working with and how many want to bring their gifts to the art of facilitating group rituals.

What are your gifts? What is your personal magic? What are the fires that are lit within you, the fires that you steward? And what are the stories that don't serve you? What falls away in the forge fire? What is the flame that is burning within you, the light that you will bring to the world?

Equinox: Planting Seeds of Rebirth

The particular magical act that is the rebirth of spring—and planting the seeds for the dreams you wish to bring into fruition—is an important part of a leader's work.

I don't know about you, but it's been a long, hard winter for me. I've been in a wrestling match with the depression that tried to take hold after my car accident in December, and I'm so grateful for the longer days and melting snow. The past month has been incredibly reinvigorating for me and I'm really ready for spring planting.

Some people are physically planting seeds at this time of year, but for most of us it's more of a metaphor. And yet, the seasons still have their pull on the ecosystem of our bodies. I often look at the time November through the silence of winter as the time to release what we really need to let go of. To identify what seeds we need to actively not plant in our garden again.

I look at New Year's Eve and the attendant New Year's Resolutions, and those months leading up to Imbolc and the Spring Equinox as the inspiration energy, preparing for new growth. Spring Equinox, then, is a fantastic time to make a solid commitment to something we've been thinking about or working with.

Spring Equinox is that fresh start, that rebirth, that time to really plant the seeds of something we want to bring into our lives.

Tarot and Rebirth
Often when we pull out the cards, we're looking for help with a decision or with choosing a direction. I know that nothing is more personally frustrating for me than when I know that I need to make a change in my life, but I feel stuck, unsure of which direction to choose. Or unsure of what's holding me back.

Tarot can be a great way to help you get at what's going on beneath the surface.

With Tarot cards—or just on your own—you might begin to consider first what you want. What are some of the goals that you dream of but perhaps haven't yet put into place? It could be actual farming or gardening, or starting a family, or changing careers, or starting a business, or starting a new community initiative or perhaps a particular creative pursuit like writing or painting. What are the things that you would like to accomplish?

You might also begin to think about what you've let fall away from your life—or what you need to let fall away. Perhaps it was a bad relationship, a toxic friend, a job that didn't serve you, a mindset about money. I've often heard that the definition of insanity is trying the same thing over and over and expecting a different result. And yet, so many people (myself included!) have gotten stuck repeating the same old things. I know that I've found myself in a few relationships that were abusive—both romantic and professional.

Often what we need to let fall away is more directly related to the pain we've suffered in the past. Call them old wounds if you like. These are the things that were done to us in our past, and we develop coping mechanisms to deal with them. And—it keeps us alive, it keeps us sane—but those coping mechanisms ultimately hold us back. In school I was emotionally, verbally, and sometimes physically abused by my peers. I toughened up, decided I didn't need anyone. I got defensive, I looked at anyone around me as an enemy. And a dozen other small coping strategies.

Literally, it kept me alive. If I hadn't done all that, the emotionally sensitive younger version of me might very well have tried to commit suicide.

But later, when I wanted to connect to people, develop friendships, nobody wanted to be my friend. I blamed it on so many things..."They don't like a fat chick. Screw them." And, that was certainly true for some of them. Yet it was also my attitude that pushed people away. I was looking at everyone I met as if they were the kids from middle school, about to hurt me. I treated people like that.

Figuring out what to let go can be the work of years. Your own meditation or journaling might help with it. Therapy can help, talking to a friend can help. Exploration through Tarot can help you see what's too close to your own face.

When you begin to release what doesn't serve you, you can then look again at what you want to bring into your life. This is where popular concepts like the Law of Attraction start to come in, but it's often oversimplified. Thinking positive is not enough–it's the way to shine the light of hope, like a lighthouse in the distance. But there's all the work that it takes to get there, all the work to release what doesn't serve you and to make room for what will serve you.

What do you want in your life? Love? Friendships? Connection? Creativity? Life Force? Abundance? I want to do what I love and get paid for it, among other things. I want to write and create art and travel and teach, and connect to other people who are doing similar work and share resources with them and build something that lasts. I want to leave the world better than how I came into it.

Ritualizing and Embodying Planting the Seeds

We humans are physical creatures. A lot of spiritual work seems to try to get us out of our bodies, but truly, are bodies are pretty powerful spiritual instruments.

When we sing, dance, and drum together, something changes. Our bodies help us to get into that trance state that can help us take the work deeper. It's one thing to think about what you need to release, or what you want to bring into your life. It's another thing entirely to embody that through singing, chanting, dancing and drumming.

Or perhaps even just to embody releasing by cutting a piece of string, or to embody bringing something into your life by burning an intention written on a piece of paper, or focusing that intention into a cup of water and drinking it.

Here is a "sketch" of a ritual that I've offered for groups at this time of year, and perhaps the words and the process will offer you some ideas for how you might physicalize setting an intention for yourself to plant the seeds of hope, of rebirth. Much of the language below is something that I might use when facilitating a ritual or ceremony for a group.

Planting the Seeds of Hope

What is often useful first is some kind of a sound purification. A singing bowl, a gong bath, singing a chant or an om. Any sound with intention can help to center and focus you.

You might also invite in any spirits, allies, or other forms of the divine to assist your work. Elements, ancestors, deities, or just honoring that you are a part of the larger universe and that the work you do to set intention has ripples throughout the fabric of that universe, whether or not you can see them.

It can also be very potent to choose a physical object to work with to represent your seed such as a stone, gem, seed, or any small object.

Can you feel and smell the season turning from Winter to Spring? The seeds begin to awaken within the earth, softening with the melting snow and rains and stretching toward the rising light. The winds of change are blowing, and the tide is turning to spring and growth and warmth and life force is rising up in our veins. What seeds do you plant, what are the dreams yet to come? What are the hopes and wishes you pray for?

As you celebrate the return of the light, breathe life into the seeds of your personal dreams. Bless the seeds of hope for healthy communities and earth sustainability. Imagine...inspire, empower, and reach for the seeds of your future.

Will you hold the seeds planted in the rich earth of your heart, and imagine the tree grown strong?

When you name your seeds you bless them. What are your dreams? What are the seeds that you plant? What are your hopes and prayers for this year? What is one big dream, a tree you would like to grow? How will you send blessings and abundance to those seeds, those dreams.

The Seed. What is the seed you wish to plant? What seeds do you plant now, or have you planted in the earth before the cold season? What are the seeds that you wish to tend for this year? For the years after?

What is the dream that you wish for? Will you dream big? What are your hopes, your wishes? When you imagine the seed, what is the plant, the tree that it will grow? What fruits will that tree bear? Standing in the place of now, can you imagine the tree grown strong and full? What is a dream that you hold? What is its scent, its taste, what does it look like or sound like? What is your dream of the future, one dream. Is it a dream of abundance, of prosperity. A dream of a new job, a dream of something you wish to learn, a new business, a new project.

Perhaps it is a maple tree, swift growing. Perhaps it is an oak tree, long to grow and long to stand. Do you hold a dream for social change, a dream of healing, a dream of a creative project? A healthy family, a healthy community?

Hold the image, the sound, the feeling. How do you hold your body here in the place where your seed has taken root and grown tall, where you can pluck the fruits of the tree. And coming back to now, when you hold the seed within your hand and your heart. What is the seed you will plant, or have planted already?

Earth
What is the soil that grows your dream? The Dreaming in the Darkness. What rich, loamy earth does your seed require to flourish? What are the nutrients your seed will need? Imagine being under the earth, in the moist darkness in the weeks and months, waiting for the thaw and waiting for the time to be right. Here is the time in the darkness, in the deep, in the waiting. When do you require darkness and silence and rest, when does that fill you and feed you?

What is the soil that will feed your dreamseed? Is it words of encouragement, is it time alone, is it the support of friends, is it financial abundance, is it family or community, what are the resources you need? What does your dream need, your seed need?

(At this time, you might plant the representation of your seed into earth, dirt, sand, or something soft.)

Water
The water that softens the seed. Can you remember being under the earth, can you remember that darkness going on and on, the winter not letting go? What is it like to be so ready for light and heat and

moisture? Have you ever been under the earth for what felt like a thousand years of darkness? And then....the waters came.

Can you remember what it felt like to have the waters touch the edges of the seed, the edges of your skin. The waters soften the seed, prepare it to grow. Can you remember the warm rains flowing down to cleanse you, prepare you?

Have you known joy or known sorrow? Why do you care about this seed? Have you felt the rains falling down on you? Or were they the waters of the stream or the lake or the ocean? How did the waters flow? Do you remember feeling? What brings life to your seed? What do you love?

Did your heart break? The Sufi say the heart must break to make more room for God to enter. When did your heart break? Where is the love inside of you, are you in love with this seed and this dream? Can you feel the waters of your love softening the edge of the seed, filling the cup of your heart, slaking the thirst of this growing plant as it grows and grows?

How do you feel? What feelings bring life to this dream seed, to this tree that will become?

(You might bathe your hands in water here, or even pour water over yourself.)

Fire

The sunlight, the fire. What is the sunlight that feeds your plant, brings it life force and vitality? What is the will that rises within you?

Fire will be the sun and the light, the Will to make the dream happen, what lights us up. What gets you on fire? What sparks your imagination? What causes the fire in the head and heart, that life force shiver to rise up your spine? What gets you excited, what is your vision of the future? Can you feel it inside you, can you reach for that sunlight that will feed you?

Can you imagine that golden beautiful radiance and as it touches your leaves and your skin and you're bathed in it, it fuels you and feeds you.

(You might light a fire at this point such as a candle, or even a campfire or bonfire if you are outside. Or you might also reach your hands up toward the sun itself, reaching for that fire.)

Air
The breath of life. What is the name of the divine? I am that I am. What brings life and consciousness to this seed, what gives it its name? Will you name this dream that you are planting, will you name the tree it will become? Will you blow a name into the seed, into the wind, and commit to making this seed a reality?

Will you turn and whisper its name to someone next to you, will you tell its story and bring it to life? Will you risk naming this dream, call it forth?

And will you say aloud one thing you can do, to take a step toward making this dream happen?

(You might speak something aloud, write something down, or simply breathe into your cupped hands or blow a breath onto the earth where you planted your seed to charge it with your energy and intention.)

Fueling Your Intention
At this point in a group ritual I typically engage people in singing a chant together which builds in intensity. We sing, we dance, we play drums, until the energy of our song and movement reaches a peak. If you're doing this exercise on your own, I recommend engaging in

some kind of energetic activity in order to "fuel" the intention, the seed, that you are planting.

There are lots of ways to raise up life force. You can sing a chant or tone along with a singing bowl or a chant CD, you can go out for a run, you can go dancing at a club or a drum jam, you can rock back and forth, or do an intense workout. Heck, you can go sing a song that fits the work you're doing at karaoke. Anything that makes a sound and gets your heart rate going is generally going to lay the pattern deeper.

If you sing, sing like it matters. Sound is energy. Life force is energy. Breathing and moving is energy.

Rebirth, Planting Seeds, and Planning
When you've done the work to set an intention, the work is not yet done. There's still the long road from here–where you are right now–to there. Envisioning what "there" looks like can be a powerful motivator, and essentially strikes the "bell" that is the fabric of the universe and says, "Hey, this is my intention, this is what I want to happen." But there's all the rest of the work we have to do to get there.

Whenever I'm planning something–particularly something big that's going to require a lot of work–I make a map. I identify what I want as clearly as I can, and then I pull out all the steps I'll need to take in order to get there. It's like a to do list, only a little prettier. I can start to get a sense of what tasks need to get accomplished first so that I can progress closer to the goal. For instance, getting a web site. Finishing a book. Getting more artwork done. Planning more traveling and teaching engagements. Or even cleaning up my art studio so that I can do more painting.

While there are a lot of thankless tasks and busywork on the way from Here to There, connecting them firmly to the big goal is a way to help you visualize and stay on track. And–if you enjoy crossing things off lists as much as I do—as you get those things done, you can see yourself on the map, getting closer to that goal. Some things don't map out as well as others, but if you have a big complicated goal this can be a good way to break it down.

And it's another place where Tarot cards can come into play as you're beginning to make decisions about particular things. Tarot is a great way to look at what's going on beneath the surface, and short 1-card or 3-card pulls can tell you a lot.

I wish you the very best in reaching for all of your dreams. Happy Spring!

Desire: Reaching for the Rose

First published in Global Goddess Oracle Summer Solstice 2013 issue

Inclusivity is part of my feminist values, but hosting truly inclusive rituals can be challenging. I inherited this value from my teachers at Diana's Grove. Inclusive language, compassionate communication, accessibility....It's one thing to say, I offer inclusive ritual.

It's another thing entirely to craft rituals that accomplish this, from structure and theme through language and the ultimate impact on the participants.

Recently I hosted a Beltane ritual that exemplifies the energy of rising life force, creativity, and passion that is part of the rising solar energy of Beltane and Summer Solstice. The ritual was designed to help us reach for desire, that deeper desire that is the longing for divine communion, the deep reaching for our dreams and callings.

This ritual, and our approach, exemplified many ways to inspire a community while also being inclusive and accessible.

Sabbats and Sexuality

Just about every time I host a Beltane, someone snickers a sex joke. There's dirty laughs all around. Then I ask, "So, is anyone here trying to get pregnant and want energy for that?" Everyone goes absolutely quiet. Then I ask, "Is anyone here want energy for food you are growing?" I live in Chicago so the answer is usually no, though lately there are more urban gardeners.

But usually I determine that nobody's looking for an old-fashioned Beltane Great Rite, nobody's looking to get pregnant, and nobody's trying to bring fertility to their crops. "So, it's not really about sex, is it?"

People look a little confused.

Usually this conversation happens when I'm doing my pre-ritual talk to go through logistics and teach the chant. I use the opportunity to talk about ritual, accessibility, and inclusivity, addressing things from physical mobility to GLBTQ inclusion.

In the majority of Pagan rituals, which generally descend from some form of Wicca/Witchcraft, the norm has been to worship the heterosexual union of Goddess and God. While that makes a lot of sense for our ancestors who prayed for fertility, it hasn't left as much of a place for our LGBTQ community members to have a seat at the table of the sacred. Those who don't conform to the gender binary often feel themselves completely out of the equation when working with duotheistic ritual, i.e., rituals that celebrate the God and the Goddess as the two gender binary halves of the divine.

We Love Good Story

It's not to say that the union of Goddess and God doesn't have a place; obviously, human sexual reproduction involves two genders. It makes sense that we generally conceive of the divine through the lens of gender, but gender assumptions and cultural roles can make our rituals inherently exclusive to some. It is worth pointing out that most of the organisms on our planet actually reproduce asexually. And, though we call the Earth our mother and assign a female gender to the planet, the Earth actually has no gender, no sex organs. The Earth is our mother in the sense of being a parent, a progenitor, a life-giver, but we have no potent word for progenitor that is not gendered.

In ritual and storytelling, we use evocative language. Mother is a more evocative word than parent. The story of the God and Goddess is engaging because it's a tale we can connect with, it uses mythic and symbolic language. I think that this is in part why it's such a powerful story that has compelled so many modern Pagans over the years.

I've already worked over the years to craft rituals that include people with various physical challenges like allergies, mobility challenges, and more. But how do I find myths that honor the cycles of the season, but that are accessible to a broad spectrum of genders and sexualities?

What's Not Inclusive?
I have to first look at ritual techniques that aren't so effective. I've seen ritualists try to be inclusive; they'll tell the God/Goddess story and then say, "But if you're not looking for sexual fertility, just channel that into creativity and abundance." It's usually offered as an afterthought.

It's potentially worse with rituals focusing on the story of the Maiden, Mother, and Crone. The priestess says, "Oh, there's nothing wrong with you that you're not a mother, I'm sure you have lots of creative projects that are just like children."

Ouch.

Painful words for women struggling with fertility, women who miscarried, women who had an abortion. More often it's just the sting of the "consolation prize," but there's the covert judgment—you're not a "real" woman if you haven't given birth and raised a child.

Inclusivity is not always easy.

On the one hand, as a Pagan community leader, I've learned that you can't please everyone. However, if inclusion is my value, then I have to work harder.

For a ritual focusing on helping people connect to their desire, I have to work to find a way to help people get to communion using the evocative power of myth and story without being exclusive.

Focus on Intention
I first look at the energy I'm going for, the emotional impact I want to have on a group. For Beltane or Summer Solstice, I'm working toward energy of creativity, desire, abundance. We're raising up the fires of life force.

The energy beneath heterosexual sex is that life force…the heat of the sun warming the earth, the seeds pushing their way up out of the ground. Lust, desire, love, unity, harmony. In the poetry of Rumi, the divine is referred to as the Beloved, and the poetry makes the intimate connection of the divine as a lover.

I had a unique challenge planning a public ritual for the Chicago Pagan community, as I was facilitating a weekend class on how to lead rituals, and the ritual was the practicum.

I stumbled onto the theme while I was preparing to teach a workshop at PantheaCon with my co-facilitator River Higginbotham. River and I discussed some of the challenges of teaching ritual facilitation.

I realized that I can teach the techniques—public speaking, body language, ritual process, leading a chant that works. What I can't actually teach is the Desire. I can't teach anyone to want to be a ritualist, to yearn so bad for it that they're willing to step past all their comfort zones, all their shyness, to learn the skills they need to be a good ritual facilitator. They have to want a good ritual for their group so bad, that they're willing to get out there and risk looking goofy in front of the group. I can't teach anyone that Desire, they either have it or they don't.

However, through ritual, I could help them to find it if it was there.

Charisma, the ability to engage a group, comes from our personal authenticity, from our connection to something deeper. That authenticity allows us to facilitate rituals that truly move people emotionally. Without that Desire, we're just watching a ritualist go through the motions. They are calling the Air, but there's no power to it. The chant dies out because there's no life force coming through.

Ritual Theme
Desire. Reaching. Yearning. Lust. Not just physical lust, or the desire we have for a new television. Divine yearning. The yearning we feel to unite with the all-that-is, whether you call that Goddess, God, Divine, Holy Guardian Angel, your deepest self, or something else entirely.

I designed a ritual around opening to that desire, to love, and began looking at deities of love to work with. So many of the love goddesses were goddesses of love, sex, lust, war, and death. Venus, Aphrodite, and other goddesses of love have often been associated with the planet Venus, which traces a five-pointed star in the sky every eight years. Roses, symbols of love, have five petals. Yet in the Tarot, the Lovers is represented by the six pointed star—two overlapping triangles, fire and water, the completely balanced union of opposites. In the Kabbalistic Tree of Life, Tiphareth is at the center of the tree, representing that six pointed star, the golden rose of love, the brilliance of the sun, harmony and connection.

I envisioned roses reaching for the sun, the sun that is the rose of Tiphareth. But how to get people to really open to that desire?

Someone once told me that many shamanic ritual patterns involve what is essentially pouring out the cup of our hearts in order to fill again. If I want to fill with joy and connection, I need to release the wounds and barriers that hold me back. It's the same process in alchemical lore; to transform, first something has to be burned down to its essence through Calcination. In the Tarot, before we can open to the waters of the Star, first the Tower must burn away all the contracts and shackles that bind us.

What holds us back? What keeps us from opening to love? What keeps us from risking and reaching and desiring?

Well…what holds you back? What holds me back?

I have my baggage like anyone else. The times my heart has been broken, the times when I've had to toughen up my skin just a little bit more in order to get through an abusive situation. My heart, like many people, is scarred over by unkind words and harsh experiences. What has kept me from reaching and risking is fear. Fear of failure, fear of looking stupid. Fear of people making fun of me. And when I'm afraid, I hide. I avoid things by procrastinating.

One of my other co-facilitators of the ritual class, Steve Smith, offered his perspective on how Hades approaches Desire. "Hades hears nothing but the laments of all the things people did not do. He knows how many breaths, how many heartbeats, each of those people wasted. They wasted some of those precious heartbeats of life force with time wasted trying to live up to someone else's expectations, or being afraid of what someone would say. In the land of the unhappy dead, there is no more reaching, no more desire, no more quickening to become more than you are, to bring your dreams into being. Your breaths are gone."

What I wanted in this ritual was to help people recognize that our lives are too short to waste the time we have doing things we don't really want to do, and to reach for the things that they really did want.

The Ritual
We used the our usual pattern—a pre-ritual talk, an energetic gathering and sound purification, grounding meditation, circle casting to connect the group, elemental and other ally invocations. Students of the ritual class took roles to practice their skills, some bringing me to tears with the honesty, authenticity, and emotion they brought.

Instead of inviting in Aphrodite or Freyja or Inanna or other specific deities of love, we invited in any deities or spirits that represented love and desire to us. We sung their names together as a group. We invited the Gatekeeper known by many names. Hades, Legba, Ganesha, Hecate, the Horned One.

Our trance journey took people first into the magic of the season, the plants blooming. Then the journey took us to the places we find ourselves wandering, lost, seeking something but distracted. We crossed the desert of the sands of wasted time, we found ourselves in the wasteland. Multiple voices of our trance team asked the questions, what distracts you? What are the things you focus on instead of what you really want? What takes your time? What are you afraid of?

Steve, speaking in the voice of the Gatekeeper, spoke. "You have so many breaths of your life, and how many of them did you waste when you could have been doing the work that calls to your soul?" While Steve was working with Hades, it was less important to the group to work with Hades as a deity, than to work with the gender-neutral archetype of the Gatekeeper.

Participants were invited to take a handful of sand and pour it into a central cauldron and acknowledge where they waste their time. We asked, what is left of your time, your energy? Is that enough energy to commit to your higher calling? The answer, of course, was no. We asked people to name their fears, their distractions, all that held them back, and to release them. To reclaim the energy and time that those things sucked away. "I'm too ugly," "I'm too fat," "I'm afraid," "I'm too shy."

Once they'd released these old fears, we began to sing a chant:
Cracking open, reaching down,
Break my heart, let the light in,

We invited participants to visit six altars. We had decorated large altars, three for fire, three for water, each reflecting a different aspect of Desire.

For Fire:
- Radiance, Brilliance, Visibility
- Power and Strength,
- Desire, Passion, Vision

For Water:
- Beauty, Grace, Enchantment, Engagement,
- Service, Devotion, Dedication
- Love, Harmony, Namaste

At each altar stood one or two anchors who aspected that piece of desire, and spoke a challenge to every participant. While I specifically worked with Freyja for the altar I anchored, that wasn't as important to the participants as it was to offer them a challenge based on that facet. "Will you step into radiance, into visibility, will you acknowledge your brilliance? If you do this, you cannot become invisible again." And if they said yes, we offered them the blessings of the divine in bringing this out into the world and a token in the form of a shimmering ribbon.

As the participants returned to the center, we gathered in two lines facing across from one other person. Here was the crux of the ritual, what all the previous work had built us towards. One by one, starting on one end, each person passed through the gauntlet. The people on either side of them looked into their eyes and spoke words of support. "I love you. I believe in you. I believe in your dreams."

This would have had far less emotional impact without the work of releasing our fears, without claiming our power, our desire, our magic, first. Many were in tears to hear genuinely spoken words of love and hope spoken to them. We returned to the center to sing a chant to raise energy for our work, to fill up with life force.

I took the chant, "Ancient Mother," by Robert Gass and exchanged "Ancient Mother" for "Oh Beloved."
Oh Beloved, I hear you calling,
Oh Beloved, I hear your song,
Oh Beloved, I hear your laughter,
Oh Beloved, I taste your tears.

We drummed, clapped, and sang a slow build of energy to a peak. We opened to desire, we risked reaching for that something larger.

We asked, what enchants you, what does your soul yearn for? What do you dream of, what calls to you? Which had nothing to do with gender, and everything to do with divine communion.

Pouring Out and Pouring In
Years ago, I had to make a choice. To be held back by my fears, or to become more than I was, to become a public speaker who could lead workshops or rituals. I overcame my fear of being around dozens of

people I didn't know. I overcame my fear of being a leader, of being charismatic. I was sure that if I stepped into that power that I would be judged. People would assume that I was there to show off. Or just as gripping, my fear of forgetting my words, of failing, of them laughing at me and rejecting me.

All of these fears were worth overcoming in order to become the person I am today, but I had to desire, to reach for a possible dream, to risk it.

In the ritual, we connected to desire together, we connected to the essence of the season of rising life force, in a way that included people of all genders and sexualities. Because, that too was worth the risk for me, risking changing how I did rituals in order to live my values.

What do you want to bring out into the world? What's worth the risk?

If you want to bring ritual that is potent and inclusive, are you willing to let go of your preconceptions of what a ritual must be? Are you willing to shift some of your language, or the myths and stories you work with? Will you modify a ritual to accommodate someone who has a hard time walking, or who is allergic to incense? What are the ways our rituals are inclusive? How are they exclusive?

How can we work to make our rituals accessible, inclusive, and stirring? Do you have the desire to be inspired, and to be inspiring? What do you love?

The Longest Night: Taking Up the Sword

First published in the Global Goddess Oracle Yule 2013 issue.

There is something about the Winter Solstice that always makes me think of story of King Arthur. I probably watched the Disney cartoon "The Sword in the Stone" a few too many times.

Even though "Excalibur" is probably the Arthurian movie that is the most burned into my brain, that image of a barely teenage Arthur out in the snow, pulling the sword from that anvil during the Christmas jousting tournament has stuck with me. It was Arthurian and Celtic myth that grew my later interest in the Grail Quest.

The story of King Arthur, for me, has become the story of the struggle to be a good and ethical leader. There are so many retellings of the story, so many versions, from the old medieval texts to the Mists of Avalon and modern movies. When I teach leadership workshops, or workshops on finding your personal magic and stepping into your power, Arthur is one of the storytelling examples that I use. Inanna is another, though I tend to use the Inanna's Descent myth more for groups that need deeper, more cathartic work.

Referencing King Arthur is a little bit like referencing the Star Wars movies; I can generally count on people knowing at least a little bit about the story. And working with myths and archetypes, I have found, is a powerful way to connect people to something larger. Sometimes the story itself does a lot of the work for us, as teachers and ritualists.

How Did I End Up a Leader?
Many leaders and community members ask me questions about leadership. I'd say at least half of the people in any of my leadership classes reveal to me, "I never wanted to be a leader, but nobody else would make anything happen so I stepped in."

Guess what—neither did Arthur.

Arthur was an underdog, in most of the stories. He was raised as a servant, probably beaten up. He grew up thinking he was worthless like anyone else who wasn't of noble blood. Arthur didn't know he was secretly the son of the king. He didn't want to be the leader, didn't ask for it. But once he pulled that sword from the stone, there was no putting it back.

I think that's what so many of us in Pagan and alternative spirituality leadership go through. We didn't necessarily want to be a leader, but we wanted a group to work with. We saw a need in our community, and we stepped up.

However, the consequences are often dire. When Arthur stepped up, what happens? In some stories, half the knights rally behind him, and half begin attacking the others. Total anarchy ensues. Arthur runs away for a moment, for one Dark Night. He thinks, "I can't cope with this. I don't know how to do this."

That sounds rather a lot like the Pagan community infighting and drama that rears its ugly head all too frequently.

Merlin, the wizard of the story who is holding down the Jungian archetype of "wise old advisor," reminds Arthur that if he doesn't do it, who will? I also like to think that perhaps Merlin reminded Arthur that Arthur brings a unique perspective to the deal that no other knight, warrior, or nobleman could; Arthur has been the underdog. He understands the experience of those born without noble blood. And thus, he may be able to make life better for the lower classes.

Arthur and Knighthood
If there was a historical Arthur, he probably wasn't what we would today call a feminist, but given Arthur has made it through history and mythology as a well-beloved savior king, I think that the story promotes the value of a king who worked to make people's lives better. Certainly just by organizing the Knights and lords into the Round Table, even if it was a men-only club, he protected the common people from getting trampled in some of the infighting that happened at that time. Many stories explore how Arthur tried to bring about a more equal form of justice.

For me, the essence of being a knight is being true and ethical. It's trying to do the right thing, trying to be of service. In fact, the root meaning of the word "knight" is "to serve." When we step in as Pagan community leaders—whether that's the titular head of a group, or a volunteer helping out with setup and potluck—we are stepping in to serve a group.

For me, knighthood and sovereignty aren't about gender. Or about a suit of armor, or even a sword. I believe that any person who finds themselves on the path of the seeker, the path of the hero's journey...the path to trying to be a better person, an ethical person, a person fighting to help others and do the right thing, is taking on that role of being a knight.

The Sword, Power, and Fear

While some feminists don't like working with the masculine imagery of the sword, for me I work with it as an archetype, a word and image that has power because of its use in the stories that inspire us. These old myths, stories of Gods and Goddesses and heroes, capture our imagination. And some of the symbols in those stories are potent, like knights and swords. One of my poetry professors once referred to what he called "Hundred dollar words," words like Aphrodite, for instance, convey a wealth of images and ideas. A sword, and in specific, the Sword in the Stone, conveys an image about taking something up. Esoteric lore sometimes looks at the sword as Will, Power, or Justice.

When we take up that Sword in the Stone, whether or not we wanted it, we can't go back. We can either use the power granted us by stepping up, or we can fail to do so. We can either try to be ethical leaders, or we can fail to do so.

The word "power" is also something I've noticed many Pagan leaders have learned to be afraid of. I was in one leadership team meeting and I brought up how group dynamics and power dynamics happen. One other group leader said, "Well, let's just not have any power dynamics." What I wanted to say was, let me know when you manage to do that. We're humans. We're social creatures. We develop friendships and romantic relationships. We get angry at each other. In any small group, dynamics develop, it's not if, it's when. And it's how we work with those dynamics that decides the fate of our group.

This is how I look at the sword. Sometimes when we step into leadership, we find we have a sword in our hand. We didn't put it there. We didn't want it, but now whenever I make a gesture, there's that sword. I don't intend to wave it around, I'm not trying to threaten anyone. But because I stepped into a position of responsibility, I took on a role with power. Power is the ability to take an action, it doesn't have to mean "power over," as Starhawk would call it. It can be "power with." But—we need to learn how to do that.

Vigils, Dark Mirrors, and Personal Work
When I teach leadership workshops, eventually I reveal the secret. I can teach all sorts of leadership and communication tools, but what really needs to happen is deep personal work. We have to look into that dark mirror, look at our own shadows. My mentors at Diana's Grove used to talk about how a leader's personal baggage is usually what destroys the group, and I've found this to be pretty accurate. Many of the leaders who come to me with problems in their group are sometimes causing some of their own problems. And they don't mean to; they have the best of intentions.

And I'm a human being too. I make mistakes as a leader. I see my own issues play out in the groups I lead, I see the places where my own failings cause difficulties for the group. For instance, I'm a great visionary, but I stumble a bit without a director of operations-type of person to help organize the details.

And perhaps that, too, is why I see the Winter Solstice as a great time to do leadership work. It's that still-point, that darkness. If we take the time to actually sit in vigil, actually work with our own shadows, we can become better, healthier leaders. In fact, I think the idea of a vigil is some of the trance techniques employed by sensory deprivation and meditation. We can use darkness and silence to still our minds; too often we keep ourselves busy, too busy to actually look into the mirror of our souls and acknowledge where we, ourselves, are causing some of our own problems.

This work isn't easy, and it's work I continue to do. It's the work of a lifetime.

Longest Night
The Winter Solstice is sometimes called the Longest Night. Can you imagine what it was like thousands of years ago when the nights kept getting longer? Can you imagine huddling by the fire and wondering if the long summer days would ever return? If maybe this was the year that the nights just kept getting longer?

I often think that some of the "lost magic" that our ancestors held as oral tradition is simply science we now take for granted. What took our ancient ancestors thousands of pounds of stone to do, we now have access to on our cell phones.

What I mean by that is, if we know the cardinal directions and have general stone markings, we can tell the passing of the seasons by where the sun rises. It's a fairly easy "computer" to build, but obviously fairly labor intensive. In the modern era, we don't have a lot of fear that the days will just keep growing shorter and colder. We know that the days will get longer and spring will come. Science and history has shown this to us.

But hundreds and thousands of years ago, I can imagine waiting and wondering, hoping and praying that the sun would indeed return.

While we can't suddenly forget the science we now know, we can still use the energies of the silence and darkness of this time of year. In a way, I look at a vigil as an intentional "dark night of the soul" which can be done as solitary ritual work, or in a group. For that matter, it's also something you can explore in a process of therapy. The modern concept of shadow work owes a great deal to Jungian therapy.

Leadership and Sovereignty

Becoming a leader to me implies a responsibility to become a better person. That each one of us, whether or not we aspire to leadership, is following the path of being the hero of our own journey. But imagine the world we could live in if we each took that responsibility to be the hero, to be the knight, the sovereign. To actually look into the mirror.

Sometimes we aren't going to like what we see. We aren't always going to like what we've done in our lives. We've all made mistakes.

Stepping into personal sovereignty isn't about wallowing in the mistakes of our past, it's about looking in the mirror to acknowledge our shadows, acknowledge the work we need to do, and moving forward and trying to be better people.

Sometimes it's looking at what you've done to get what you want, vs. doing the right thing. Sometimes it's just facing the consequences of your actions and apologizing. Being a knight and being in service to something larger than just yourself isn't always easy.

For me, the story of King Arthur brings up an axiom of leadership and personal work. It's not what we do when things are easy that define us. It's the choices we make when times are tough, when our back is against the wall, when the stones of the Tower are crumbling down around us that define our ethics, our values, and our honor.

The essence of that hero's journey is that moment in the silence of your own heart when you have to look into the mirror, look at who you are, look at the "sword" in your hand, and decide if you're going to do the honorable, ethical thing or the self-serving thing. And yet, stewarding yourself and following your own calling so that you aren't betraying your own path.

The path of the leader, the knight, the sovereign is not always easy to balance. But exploring ourselves like this is so crucial to being better leaders. To being better people. To building a better world.

The Longest Night: An Arthurian Ritual and Vigil

First published in the Global Goddess Oracle Yule 2013 issue

Here is a ritual that I sometimes facilitate during leadership classes, particularly near the Winter Solstice. The core of this ritual is that each person stepping into the ritual becomes Arthur, Arthur transitioning from youth to sovereign. Each person steps into knighthood, into responsibility, whether they are an acknowledged leader in their own community or if their goal is stepping into personal sovereignty.

Pulling the Sword from the Stone may be something they did by accident or by intention, but either way, they can't put it back, and so their work is to face their shadows, to become more than they are, to become their best selves.

The specifics of how sacred space is set up can vary quite a bit depending upon your specific spiritual tradition. My ritual work is ecstatic and extemporaneous and leans upon the general format of

Reclaiming rituals. Here's how I might approach it, but this can all be adapted.

Pre-ritual talk: Identify the theme of the ritual, teach any chants, let people know any physical logistics beforehand.

Gathering: Use chanting and rhythm to draw the group together.

Grounding/Centering: Let the participants connect to their deeper selves through a brief meditation, weaving in some of the themes of the ritual. Imagining being Arthur on the night before their vigil. Hearing the silence of the snow. Listening to the sound of their own pulse, their heartbeat.

Circle: Here is where I bring them into connection as a group. For this particular ritual I work with the 12 signs of the Zodiac as 12 Knights of the Round Table, 12 challengers. So I might invite everyone to imagine the dome of the heavens above us, the stars, and beyond that, the circle of the wheel of the year, each sign passing across the sky until we've come full circle. That there are 12 signs, just like there are 12 numbers on a clock face, and that we each contain all of these signs within us. That this is the circle that contains the work of our group. I might then invite each person to speak their name into the circle to acknowledge their presence, to affirm that they are ready to step into this work together. Speaking our names is powerful intentional work.

Elemental invitations: I've done this a few different ways with this ritual, depending on how many volunteers I have. One ritual, I called people forward by the signs broken down by element; I called the Air signs of Gemini, Libra, and Aquarius, and so forth. However, typically if I'm having people visit various altars/stations during the ritual, I work to metaphorically and conceptually "build" those during the elemental invocations.

Air: Speaking our intention, claiming it aloud. Also, acknowledging the words we have spoken in anger, the words we regret, and the words others have spoken to us to diminish our power. Taking responsibility for our words going forward, acknowledging the power of our words.

Fire: Being Knighted, claiming our power, claiming our will, standing up.

Water: Anointing, acknowledging the compassion of the leader, the cup of our own hearts, the emotional connection to those we serve.

Earth: Knightly belt, the physical representation of the privilege it is to be a leader, to serve others.

Center: The central fire that drew us together, the call that we followed, the call to our destiny that rang out across the worlds and echoed back and brought us here into this place.

Ancestors and Descendants: The reason we must step into being our very best selves. We take inspiration from the ancestors before us who helped us to get where we are, while acknowledging the mistakes of the ancestors that made our own road harder. And we look forward to our own descendants of blood and of spirit. Will we make their road harder, or easier?

Arthur: We invite in Arthur, the hero, into each person.
Merlin and the Lady of the Lake: The wise guardians and guides who help us along the path.
The 12 signs of the Zodiac: Doing a long invocation/invitation of each of the 12 signs would take quite a while, so I work to do these quickly, or as I mentioned above, grouped by element.

Storytelling and Trance Journey: Here I offer context via telling a story, but the story becomes a trance journey when I move from "Let me tell you about King Arthur" to, "And when have each of you been Arthur? When did you pull the sword from the stone?"

Here is some language I might use:

"Listen to the falling snow…The longest night calls us to our vigil. Will you light the Yule fire to summon the returning sun? We gather together out of the cold to light this communal fire. Do you remember what it was like to gather to hear stories around the fire? Here is the tale of King Arthur, who began as a youth serving in the household of a knight, a noble lord…"

After telling a brief (2 minutes) version of the tale of King Arthur, or at least, part of the story, I bring it into a Trance Journey where multiple voices are speaking simultaneously to bring participants into a deeper trance state.

"When did you pull the sword from the stone? When did you change your destiny by intention or accident? When have you been the hero, the dreamer? Perhaps you, like Arthur, beheld a vision, a midwinter dream for your kingdom. Yet, to be a Sovereign, first you must become anointed as a knight. You are Arthur. You are the hero. Will you begin this journey? Will you face the challenges of the 12 Knights of the Round table, the 12 Astrological signs of the Zodiac. Will you seek Knighthood, personal excellence, integrity…in order to bring back the light to the dreams you hold, to bring the light to our own community?"

Sometimes I offer this as a "walking trance" where people walk slowly and softly around the central fire. Other times I invite people to make themselves comfortable, to trance with their eyes opened or closed.

"Arthur, you sit in vigil on the longest night. At dawn, you will be knighted. What is it like to sit here in the silence, in the waiting? What thoughts move through your mind?"

After spending some time to build that experience,

"And here as you sit, you are visited by your two mentors. Merlin and the Lady of the Lake. They have words for you, a challenge. They tell you of the challenges you will face, of the knights who will, at times, stand against you. And that those nights stand within you. They begin to guide you through a journey to face the twelve knights, the twelve challengers of the Zodiac."

In fiction writing, I've heard this technique called a double frame or a windowing; we're taking participants on a journey as Arthur, and then Merlin and the Lady of the Lake are taking Arthur on a journey. It serves to deepen the trancework.

"Arthur, you will face many challengers, and the first is Aries, the challenge of Self. Who are you? When have you put your own Self in front of others? When have you not known who you are? When have you seen others put their self and in front of others?"

The trance journey takes the participants through some of the unique challenges of each sign of the Zodiac. It can be a fun exercise to work through this and come up with your questions, and it'll help you learn a lot about astrology if you aren't already familiar.

I've also facilitated this ritual by taking a very quick (verbal) journey through the 12 signs, and then having 12 altars ringing the room/grove of trees, grouped by element, so really, having 4 elemental "zones." Participants traveled around to all 4 zones. At each zone, I would either have one person anchor all 3 elemental signs, asking challenge questions for each, or, 3 people in each zone asking challenge questions related to the sign they are representing. It depends greatly on how many ritualists I have as volunteers.

However, ritual roles like this are a great way for new ritualists to step into public speaking, since they are working with 2-3 people at a time instead of the whole group. In a larger ritual where I have 12 people for each of the signs, I'm not going to be able to anoint/knight everyone at the end because doing that one-on-one for 50-100 people would take forever.

Usually when I'm doing the version of this ritual with the longer trance journey, and with less participants and volunteers, I might have 4 elemental activities to acknowledge their knighthood toward the end of the ritual. I might transition from the trance with, "And now, to claim your knighthood, you can go to the altar of water, to be anointed and blessed by the Lady of the Lake. You can go to the altar of fire, to be knighted with the sword by being tapped on the shoulder. And you can go to the altar of air, to speak a promise, or to have witnessed words and thoughts that must be released. But first, let us acknowledge Earth, with the knightly belt."

One activity that works well is using strands of white yarn or ribbon; I have pre-cut the strands and have them available in a large bowl, and each person can take one. I might say, "In times of old, the symbol of a knight was a white belt, a white girdle. I invite you to tie these strands around your wrist if you wish, and to tie knots of blessing into each other's strands." If elemental associations aren't important you don't need to use them. Whether people are visiting 12 Zodiac altars/challengers, or 3 altars while tying blessing knots into each other's strands of ribbon, I have people holding the space and focus with a simple chant.

**An important note for this ritual: if you are working with actual swords, you need to address that in your pre-ritual talk. In my case, I have a large sword but it is unsharpened. I've also worked with a scythe for a Samhain ritual. I don't let people handle swords, scythes, or knives in ritual unless I know them very well, and I make that clear. I also offer the choice that if people aren't comfortable being tapped by the sword, that they can acknowledge their own knighthood without the tapping of the sword, that they are empowered to do so.

Transition to Energy Raising: When everyone has finished and we return to the center, I transition the group. It gives them a few moments of a break between singing the chant we've used to hold space before we sing a chant to raise energy.

I might say, "Arthur, each of you, Arthur," while looking into their eyes, "Are you a knight?"
And they say, "Yes!"
"Arthur, are you a sovereign?"
And they say, "Yes!"
"Arthur, as a sovereign, a knight, a hero…as a leader stepping in, as a leader taking responsibility, as a servant to community, what is the work you wish to do in this world? What is the dream? What is your dream?"

I work to get the group willing to speak their intentions aloud. Sometimes one at a time, in a small group, sometimes layering and overlapping in a larger group.

"Arthur, what is the sacred fire in your heart? Will you sing now for that dream? Will you sing for the returning sun, the returning light? Will you sing now, all of you, as knights of the Round Table, as servants of destiny and community, as servants of that dream and of a brighter world? Will you sing for that sacred fire, the fire of your dream, the fire of the returning light?"

After that, I (or another chant anchor) will begin to sing the energy-raising chant. There's a few chants I commonly use for this, but the idea is to use an energetic chant that is also simple enough that the group can easily learn it. Adding in harmonies, drums, vocal percussion, and movement can work to build the energy to a peak—typically ending on just a harmonic tone/singing bowl sound.

Benediction: In the stillness after we have sung and danced, one ritualist offers a summary of what we did together in the ritual. That might be something like,

"We sang together. We sang for each other's hopes, each other's dreams. We sang for the world we want to see. We sang for each of us to have the power to make a difference in the world, to hold compassion and strength in our heart. To stand up and be the leaders our community needs. Here in this place, will you once again speak your dream, your intention?"

And people speak.

Depending on the group, I might push them further into community cohesion with:

"Each of us sang. We sang for our own dreams, but we sang together. I sang for my dreams, and I sang for your dreams. I sing for your dream," and I look at one of the people across from me, and then another, "I sing for your dream," and people usually catch on after I do that for a few people and begin looking around the circle, speaking the words "I sing for your dream" to each other. That eye contact at the end of a ritual is an excellent way to help a community forge stronger connections.

It's particularly useful if these are people who are local to each other but who haven't formed a strong group yet, or leaders who may have had challenges with each other in the past.

When the group is ready, we thank the energies/deities/archetypes we invited in. I don't call these "dismissals" because in my own path I don't believe I have the power to summon something, much less command it to leave, so instead I invite the presence, and thank the presence at the end.

Using This Ritual

This ritual works well for people who have already stepped in as leaders to begin to identify their deeper work, but it also works for people who are new to the idea of leadership or who aren't quite comfortable calling themselves leaders. As you can see, it's a ritual that can be adapted for different traditions, and you can even adapt it for something like private trance work on your own. Whatever myth you work with, I believe that stories and archetypes can be a powerful guide into our own dark mirrors. When we look at our shadows, when we work to heal our past and acknowledge our shadows, we can become the leaders our community needs.

RITUAL FACILITATION

Art, Ritual, Performance, and Transformation

First published in Pantheon, A Journal of Spiritual Art

What is the difference between a ritual and a performance piece? What makes something installation art and something else a shrine, altar, or temple? When is our singing sacred and when is it just entertainment? When is a painting just aesthetic, and when is it a connection to the deep and transcendent?

I have struggled with these questions for some time. For me, painting is so often an act of devotion. Sometimes it is through my subject matter that I explore the divine, such as when I paint images like the Grail, the World Tree, the Sacred Fire, the Lotus.

Sometimes it's the act of painting itself that puts me into the zone, into a trance state, where I feel myself losing that separation between me/my local self/my identity, and the larger all-that-is.

In recent years as I've led large group rituals, I've begun asking deeper questions. What is performance, what is sacred, what is art, and when is there a difference? In many rituals I facilitate for the Earth-centered, Pagan, and alternative spirituality community, I decorate the space. As we are typically renting a space instead of using a devoted church or temple space, I work hard to set up altars, candles, archways, and other mental triggers that we are stepping into sacred work.

But these could just as easily become installation pieces.

When people take on roles in rituals, they might invite in one of the elements of Air, Fire, Water, or Earth, or invite in the ancestors, deities, or other archetypes. They might stand near an elaborate altar and speak in the voice of Apollo or Lugh or Brigid or Freyja or the Horned One.

But these could just as easily be performances.

What is the difference? And what makes them the same?

For me, part of the difference is intent. If I host a performance art/installation art event with altars—installation art—for each of the 12 signs of the Zodiac, and have 12 performers speaking in the voice of each of the 12 signs, the people attending might not perceive this as spiritual or religious, just as entertaining. They are not approaching the 12 installations as shrines, they are not stepping into temple space, they are simply observing an art piece which may or may not transform them.

However, for me, transformation is what makes these two things the same. I am a mystic, in that I believe I have experienced direct communion with the divine. I am agnostic inasmuch as I don't pretend to understand the depths of the divine, or how the divine might manifest for you or anyone else. As a ritualist, I use ecstatic techniques like singing and dancing to help the group get into a trance state so that they can commune with the divine in whatever way works for them, in whatever form works for them. I'm not there to teach a theology, I'm just there to get people to the door. It's the role of the priest/ess, the shaman, the witch.

But as an artist, I can take people to that door, even if they aren't calling it spiritual or divine. Whether you are engaging in this piece as a ritual, or as an installation/performance piece, imagine this experience:

You have entered a building where you are greeted. You are asked to pass down a hallway which has veils you must pass through; they are soft and silky. There is gentle drumming being played, and there are people speaking, their voices overlapping.

"What is your journey? What is your destiny?" "Who are you, who would you become?" "What has brought you here to this moment?" "What has held you back from being..." "Being who you could be," "Reaching for a dream," "Stepping into your power." "What has made you powerless? When have you lost your way?" "What has distracted you, what has called you away?"

The questions overlap and overlayer with the drumming as you pass along through the hallway until you come into a large room. There are people wandering around from one area to the next; it looks like there are about 12 shrines or installations. People stand and listen to costumed performers speak. At some places, they light something on fire. At others, they submerge something in water.

Someone in an elaborate robe stands before you. "You may enter the Temple of the Zodiac. You may visit as many shrines as you wish to listen to the wisdom of the twelve astrological signs. When you are finished, you may exit there."

You are allowed to pass. You go to the closest area; there is a man lounging on a decadent chaise, there is greenery all around him and a table heaped high with food. "I am Taurus," he says. "I like my comforts. Don't you? What are your comforts? What are the physical pleasures you just can't live without?" You think about it, not sure if you should answer.

Nobody else standing there speaks. "Oh, come now. What are those pleasures that you just crave. Is it chocolate?" One person nods. "A nice comfy bed? Or a couch?" A few others nod. "What about sex? What would you do for some really great sex? Or what have you done," he grins. He rattles off a few other comforts until he strikes a nerve. Yes, that is the physical comfort that always seems to take a precedent.

"How have these comforts held you back? When have they kept you from reaching and risking to do the work that truly calls to your soul?" You can think of a lot of times when you gave up your dream for this comfort. You wonder how he knew. "Here, here is a bit of ash. When you are ready, take up a handful. Think about how you are attached to some comforts, how they rule you. How they shackle you. When you are ready, release them here into the earth," he gestures at a huge vat of soil with plants that is at his feet. You take the ash in your hands, you think of the time you've wasted on something that is ultimately meaningless, when you could have instead pursued your passions. You release the ashes into the ground, and Taurus smiles at you. "The earth receives your sacrifice, the earth breaks your chains."

You wander to other altars, to the fiery bright altar of Leo. It seems there are a hundred candles bedecked around Leo garbed in red and orange and gold. Leo sits enthroned before a blazing fire. "Come forth," she demands. "You are here to see me. To witness me. Do you not see how special I am, how unique?"

She smiles, pausing. "Do you think I am selfish? Do you think I am a show-off? Perhaps it is because each one of you fears that deep inside, if you let yourself, you would be a show-off too. When have you been so consumed with being seen and being special that you demanded a group's attention? When are you the show off? And did it feel good or were you guilty about it? Perhaps you are the one who needs to be right all the time, needs to make other people wrong. Is that you?"

You actually blush, thinking about the times when you were a know-it-all, when someone would talk about something and you'd interject, "Actually, you're wrong, this is how that works." Was that it, was it a need to be seen and special? You just wanted people to like you for being smart, but it never seemed to work out that way. But you didn't stop doing it. You'd press the point further. A lot of people you once called friend seem to avoid you after you've told them how wrong they are.

Leo is speaking again; she strolls around with a feathered fan, wafting it near people's faces. You realize her skin is painted gold. "Don't we all want to be seen? Don't we all want to be special? But how do we act out in a way that annoys others? When are we showing off? Can we perhaps find a better way? Each of us deserves to be seen, to be special, to be unique. How are you unique?"

People begin speaking. "I'm an artist," one says, "I'm a writer." "I'm a mother." "I help communities in need." "I rescue animals." The words flow out, and you find yourself speaking your own truth, what you wish everyone would see about you. "I'm smart, I'm competent. I'm good at things." You know that you just wish people would acknowledge it without you having to put on a show. Leo looks into your eyes and nods.

"You are smart, and competent, you are good at things. Now, how can you find a way to be seen, and ask to be recognized, that helps people to see that? And would you release the other ways, the showing off that does not serve?" She hands you a slip of paper. "What old ways of being seen do not serve you? Release them into the fire. Begin anew." People cast their pieces into the fire.

You have visited all of the shrines, and you pass through the veils of the exit. More voices, more drumming. "What do you seek? What have you always wanted to become? What have you let fall away?" The voices overlap, and you can hear a song being sung. You enter another room with a fire in the center, and people are collected together around the fire, singing this song. It's repetitive, a chant. Another person in an elaborate gown stands before you. "You may join the music in the center; you may sing and add your voice, or you may also just sit on the edge and listen to the music."

The music in the center shifts to a tone, and silence, and then there is the rising sound of a gong bath, the sound is overwhelming. You take a seat, letting the sound wash over you and fill you. It is like the crashing sound of the ocean, it is a larger sound than you have ever heard. When the sound fades away, someone begins another song and people join them. The rhythmic song is easy enough that you join in, you find yourself drifting toward the fire in the center where others stand, swaying.

Others simply stand on the edge and watch, and others slowly leave the room. When you have sung until your voice is too sore to continue, and that song falls to silence, you leave the room and find yourself in the outer lobby of the event space.

You think about all you have seen and experienced. You think about the changes you might make in your life, the way you want your life to be, not the way it is, always scrambling to catch up on bills and paying for things you don't really need on credit cards, hiding your true feelings from the people around you, never really connecting. You want something more. You're not sure quite what that will look like, but you wonder that you never thought of that before, that nobody ever told you there was something more out there. That your life could be different. You feel shaken up but in a good way.

***

Imagine that experience. It could be a ritual, it could be an art installation. But it can lead to our personal transformation. For me, there is no separation between spirituality and the art of transformation. As someone who is a Pantheist and a bit of an Archetypist, I believe in an immanent divine that is in all of us. In ecstatic ritual, I work to connect people to the all that is, to the am-that-I-am, to the divine within and without, however that looks to them. It could be God, or a God or Goddess, or a spirit or element or an ancestor, it could be a holy guardian angel or an inner divine. It could just be that something larger, that universe out there that we are just cells of, atoms of.

I believe that the spiritual work that I do is the art of helping people to transform their consciousness. To release the old patterns and behaviors that no longer serve us, to reach for what we've always wanted. To live a life of meaning. To achieve this, I use ecstatic ritual techniques. Technologies, I call them. It's really just science. Multiple voices speaking at once. Drumming. Singing. Movement. Layered experiences that increase in emotional depth. These are all very old technologies that the oldest traditions have used for thousands of years.

But beyond the science there is magic. I usually define magic as science we don't yet understand, but here I mean magic as that something deeper, that something that defies words. It's the sensation mystics have when they commune with the divine. We can't put our experience into proper words. We try. Read Rumi or Hildegaard von Bingen to see the fumblings and attempts to explain that communion.

When we sing, dance, drum, when we create a painting or sculpture, when we experience a play, we have the capacity to touch that something larger. Name it what you want, but it is compelling and continues to call to us in many forms. As artists, as ritualists, as seekers, we can help bring people to that place of connection, whether they call it a spiritual experience or just transformation.

What transforms you? What art, dance, song, play has send the shiver down your spine, has caused you to question what you are doing in your life? What song has brought you to tears? What does divine communion feel like for you?

Section Four: Advanced Skills in Ritual

Ritual Design & Facilitation: Coping with Ritual Disasters

There are so many things that can go wrong during or before a ritual...and then there's you, the leader. The one who has to make it happen. You don't get to go into the corner and cry. Instead, you get to step up and step in. I thought that I'd share some of the more difficult experiences I've had facilitating rituals and how I got through it.

I'll touch a bit on self care and when it really is time to bow out or cancel, however, most of the time those of us who step into facilitating rituals are going to just have to get it done, even if we aren't in the mood.

Ritual Purification and Preparation
While teaching a 2-day ritual arts intensive in Chicago, several people asked me, "How do you prepare for ritual?" "How do you purify? Do you take a bath, work with herbs, or meditate?"

I think I know what they're asking; they have stage fright and they want a magical technique to banish their fear and help them become Super Ritualist. Unfortunately, it's not something I can give them.

Here's the truth; when I'm facilitating a ritual at a festival, or when I'm hosting a day-long event in Chicago, I am hopping busy the entire time. I might get to use the restroom if I'm really lucky. So no, I don't do any special grounding or meditating. I just take a breath, get out there and do it. Now—with years of practice, you won't need much preparation either. Public speaking gets easier.

Once upon a time I was an incredibly nervous facilitator, so if having a process of a meditation helps you with where you're at right now, there are some energetic techniques in Michelle Belanger's "Psychic Energy Codex" to help you focus. Any chakra or other meditation that helps you feel centered can work.

However, on thinking about those questions, I realized that I'm no longer nervous when facilitating is because I've been through some real ritual disasters, and keeping calm saved me every time.

Break-Up Before Ritual
The morning of an important ritual I was hosting in St. Louis, my live-in boyfriend broke up with me. A year before, he had joined the leadership team of the group I was co-organizing. We wanted to host a larger event so I spearheaded organizing a day-long Pagan conference. Five tracks of workshops, catered food, evening ritual, local presenters, out-of-time presenters...it was a huge event.

And it would have been great, except it was in January and an ice storm hit 12 hours before the event. Half our presenters couldn't even get into town. We were out around $2,000. A month later, our group hosted the ritual portion of the event as a benefit and we gathered auction items by the armful.

My boyfriend had taken several key ritual roles, plus he was supposed to help me load my van and do physical setup. He had unmedicated Bipolar and his mood swings had gotten worse. When I woke up the morning of the fundraiser ritual, he broke up with me.

When I left for the event venue, he was still in a full meltdown. However, I had an obligation to fulfill my role as the lead organizer for the fundraiser. I arrived at the venue and told my team, "_____ broke up with me so he won't be joining us. I'll restructure the ritual. Please don't hug me, I'll cry later." Folks respected my boundaries. We got it done, and we raised the money we needed.

This was one of my first experiences stepping in as a lead ritualist. I had a great team, but I had taken on spearheading the event, so I was the energy-driver. I didn't get to curl up and cry. And I didn't have time to purify or freak out about talking in front of 80 people. I just had to get out there and be charismatic and engaging so that we'd raise enough money to cover our costs.

Ever since then, I haven't needed any preparation to step into ritual. I think that the Tower burning down around me that day set fire to the last of my public speaking fear. There just wasn't room for it after that.

Ritual with a Concussion
This story might be more entertaining if I actually got the concussion in the ritual I was co-facilitating. I had food poisoning the day before the ritual, then passed out in the bathroom and hit my head on the floor. I didn't know it until later when I kept getting the spins, but I'd given myself a concussion. It really never occurred to me to go to the hospital and get checked out as I don't have health insurance.

The next morning I had a black eye. Fortunately, I had friends on the ritual facilitation team with heavy-duty makeup. This was another big fundraiser ritual, as it happens, raising money to preserve the forest south of Diana's Grove that was in danger of being clear-cut.

What was actually more stressful for me at the time was shenanigans going on with the leadership team I'd joined in Chicago. I'd joined a Pagan networking initiative in Chicago. Unfortunately, the entire team except for the main leader bitterly resented me being added for several complicated reasons, largely that the main leader hadn't asked their permission. The team boycotted the fundraiser ritual and demanded a meeting in a neutral location early the next morning.

I got over the food poisoning and though I felt vaguely unwell, during the ritual I just sort of went into the "doing ritual" zone and I felt fine. The meeting the next morning was more challenging as I had to deal with a very awkward situation without losing my temper. In fact, that meeting—and one of the confrontations—goes into the category of "Things I couldn't make up if I tried," but that's a story for another day.

The point being, I felt really crummy, and I still did the work I'd committed to.

It's on Fire!
I am prone to the ritual axiom, "When in doubt, set it on fire." My friend and co-facilitator Steve Smith has said that my tagline should be "We Need More Candles."

But there's a good reason—a fire in the center of the room is a powerful way to center and focus a group. And as I've said in my chanting article, if you're having trouble getting people chanting, light a fire; it's literally twice as hard to get people chanting or dancing without fire.

Yet, fire safety is important too. Here are a few accidents I've encountered, and how I worked through them.

I've only set myself on fire in ritual once. I had a scarf with silk fringe. And I swear, I was only lighting four votive candles. I was lighting one votive on each corner of the square table. I lit the first votive, and leaned over to light the second...and you can probably see where this is going.

When I registered the fire, my brain went into problem-solving bullet points:
- Altar on Fire: No
- Shauna on Fire: Yes
- Can Shauna put fire out—

Before I'd fully processed the third point, reptile brain had decided that my right hand was going to reach up, grab the scarf in the middle, and give it one good solid flick. The fire was out. I was more surprised by my hand moving without my permission than I was by the fire. None of the participants even noticed what was happening— and they didn't need to. I smiled and kept going with the ritual, because screaming wouldn't have served the group. Your ability to keep calm in a crisis helps everyone keep calm.

Cauldron Fire Fail
I once had a participant fall chest-first into a cauldron fire (one of the rubbing alcohol fires in a cast-iron cauldron). We were singing the final energy-raising chant. The fire was low to the ground, she was suddenly wildly, crazily dancing on a very shiny wooden floor really close to the fire. When she fell, I somehow got down next to her, pulled her back, and was patting her down before I realized she wasn't actually on fire. But the group, of course, all took a collective gasp/shriek. The chant ground to a halt.

I looked at the woman. "Are you ok?" I asked.
She nodded. "I'm fine."
So I looked at everyone else there. I said, "Are you guys ok? Let's all take a breath."

And we did. Then I said something else to transition them, something like, "Let's take a moment to collect ourselves, to recenter our energies here on this season, to remember and respect this fire that stands in our center, to come together," and I invited everyone in closer. I knew getting them to sing a complicated chant after that was a facilitation mistake, but just ending the ritual without any energetic resolution would have been jarring. "Let's sing a tone together to hold the energy, and let it continue and rise," and we began a rolling Om, slowly increasing the volume until it then fell to silence. Then I went through the process of closing out the ritual.

If the participant who fell had been injured, we'd of course have been calling 9-11 instead.

It wasn't until later that I learned that the participant who fell into the fire had been stalking one of my ritual team members all night. While he was knighting people—with a sword—she actually whipped out her cell phone to get his number and ask him out. (Really, I can't even make this stuff up.)

This would have been a disaster with a less safe fire; the alcohol/cauldron fires are great because it's actually fairly difficult to catch on fire from them. Ritual pro-tip: Keeping calm is good. But, identifying unstable people is also important—later this participant engaged in continually disruptive behavior. There are ways to mitigate that in a public ritual, though that's an article all its own. Another pro-tip: Have people flagged for fire safety. Keep a wet towel under your altar table or nearby. With a rubbing alcohol fire that's usually all you need to put the fire out.

Altar on Fire
I was in Memphis at Festival of Souls doing their main ritual working with Hestia, Hecate, Hephaestus: the fires of the Hearth-tender, the Lantern Light, and the Forge-Worker. During the ritual, participants were to process around the room to the different altars and engage in a journey which ultimately took them back to the fire in the center while musical guests SJ Tucker and Heather Dale led them in a haunting chant.

I'd set up cauldron fires on the two side altars/journey stations. On one the rubbing alcohol leaked out of the small cauldron. There was a small hole I hadn't noticed when I tested it, and the alcohol saturated the altar cloths. Once the fumes reached one of the lit votives on the table, it ignited.

We had just finished inviting the Elements and were about to invite in the Deities/Archetypes when I hear, "Fire! Altar's on fire!" There were 100 people clustered around me so the altar wasn't in my immediate line of sight.

Three people were trying to put the fire out. Two were removing the lit votives, and one had just pulled off the (unlit) smaller cauldron as it was the cloth beneath it on fire. I walked over and folded the altar fabric over itself twice, extinguishing the fire. Several folks worked to put out all the votives and take the now stinky fabric outdoors while I returned to refocus the group.

"Let's all take a breath," I said. (It's a great catch-all facilitation phrase for transitions.) I was invoking the three deity/archetypes with a chant, so shifting the energy back wasn't too difficult once the crisis was averted. This accident wouldn't have happened if I'd 1. Tested that cauldron more thoroughly and found the tiny hole, and 2. If I'd had a metal plate under the cauldron like I usually do.

Ultimately, this is why I use rubbing alcohol fires. There were four layers of fabric on that altar; only one was burned, and not a mark on the table. Rubbing alcohol is easy to put out if there is an accident.

Ritualist pro-tip: if you're using fire, practice first. You need to know how it works, or work with a responsible fire-tender. Once I was supporting someone else's ritual on a campus field, and they set up a small grill with broken legs. They used a bunch of sticks with lamp oil for accelerant. A huge blaze went up. No, they didn't have permission to use fire. We had no water except for my water bottle, which I used to douse the burning grass around the grill. Later, there was a singed square in the middle of the field like an alien ship had landed.

Don't let an unskilled pyro do your fire. Of the hundreds of rituals I've attended or led, I'm giving you the very rare fire accidents I've encountered, all of which were manageable because 1. I know how to put a fire out and 2. I keep calm.

Responsibility vs. Self Care
Sometimes you have to just keep calm and step in and do the ritual. Sometimes, you have to make the responsible decision to not do the ritual or event. It's a tough call.

Sometimes it's worth pushing yourself because you committed to doing something and whatever the cost, you have a responsibility to be there. If I'm the core organizer, I don't get to just not show up because I'm sick. When my old car broke down on the way to several events, I did what I had to do to get there. On the way to the 2010 Pagan Spirit Gathering, my engine overheated, my tire deflated, my brakes went out, and my fuel filter broke. It took me 3 days for an 8-hour drive. But I committed to doing the main ritual and I so I got there.

Other times I've made sacrifices in order to do something that I committed to and self-care might have been a better option. It's worth asking, "What's the cost if I push that hard?"

Cancelling the St. Louis event because of that ice storm is one of the hardest decisions I've ever made. It completely demoralized our team. But it was the right call for safety reasons. When my father died, I was supposed to teach in Rockford that weekend, and I rescheduled the event later that year. That was a reasonable thing to do.

Maybe the disaster is a fire, or maybe it's your mental state. Maybe it's the weather, or your car, or a bad phone call with your mom, or

Sharknado. Whatever the challenge is, if you're the core anchor, most of the time you're going to have to button up and make it happen.

Nothing is ever made better by freaking out. If you're the core organizer, your composure makes others calm. You shape and direct the energy of the group.

Ritual Design & Facilitation: Planning Festival Rituals

So you've been asked to lead a ritual at a Pagan Pride or other festival. Maybe you've run public rituals before, but you know this will be a little different. Or maybe you've run rituals like this and gotten frustrated when they don't turn out the way you intended. Or perhaps you have found yourself aggravated when you and the festival coordinator had very different expectations about the ritual.

Your ritual is at noon in the unrelieved sun. It's 100 degrees. What do you do?

Many of the challenges can be addressed by getting answers to core questions, like: How many people will be there? What is the ritual area like? Are there any special traditions you'll need to include? This article came about from a conversation I had with ritualist Johnny Rapture, as well as from questions from workshop attendees when I teach at Pagan conferences.

I can honestly say that some of the hardest work that I do as a ritualist is to facilitate a ritual at a Pagan Pride event, and it's probably not for the reasons you think.

Baseline Challenges

For someone used to leading rituals for 5-20 people, 30-50 could instill serious public speaking fear. Plus, there are the ritual logistics challenges that I've addressed in previous articles—having people line up one-at-a-time can work for a group of 20, but not for 50-500. Not without significant modification.

For my part, that crowd of 500-500 people doesn't bother me. And, I know enough about scaling physically-inclusive ritual pieces that I can adapt to a range of group sizes. What's more challenging is that I don't have control over almost any of the logistics of space—where the ritual is held, and timing—how long I have.

Expectations

I'm often supposed to adhere to a number of guidelines, but festival organizers aren't always great at communicating those. If you've ever organized a Pagan event, you know that event organizers are busy people. In fact, just because someone is organizing an event, they may never have facilitated a ritual and might have no idea what you need to know.

Similarly, a festival organizer might have expectations about how you'll do a ritual but, as so often goes with expectations, they may not even realize they have them. An organizer may not be able to communicate their assumptions until you send them an outline of your plan and they say, "Oh, no, that will never work because you need to do ____." Or worse—after the ritual they say, "We've never done it that way. I'm very disappointed."

As a facilitator you may have expectations about how a ritual area will be prepared, and then arrive to find out that there isn't really a dedicated ritual space. However, you also never asked the event coordinator about that. In fact, many of the conflicts that I witness come from expectations that were never communicated.

Specific Logistics Challenges

The most difficult rituals I facilitate are at Pagan Pride events—I want to get people deep and I'm hamstrung. Most of the techniques I use, I cannot employ. In previous articles I've written about some of the different techniques I use to get people into that altered state of consciousness where they can do deeper spiritual work. Decorating the space, dimmed lighting, using a central fire, making sure it's a private space where people feel safe, and taking enough time to get people into the groove...

At a Pagan Pride, I have access to probably none of that. A while back, a friend of mine who had attended one of my rituals said, "I'm running an event like a Pagan Pride and I'd like for you to come out and do our ritual. Can you do one that's all deep and cathartic and intense like what you did at XYZ event?"

And I had to be honest. "No," I said. "I can't." And I outlined why. A number of the reasons are contained in the below list. All of these are fairly typical features of a ritual at a day-long Pagan fest like Pagan Pride:

- Ritual area is out in a big open space without shade, or
- Ritual is in a big noisy vending hall
- Ritual area has poor sound containment—no tree cover, or next to a soccer game, or next to a road with cars going by, or by a sound stage with music blasting
- There might be non-Pagans standing around and observing, and also Pagans who don't want to participate, but instead hang back and just watch
- Usually you can't use fire, and it's out in the bright daylight anyways
- There's no way to please everyone, particularly when facilitating for people of many different traditions
- You can't plan for the number of attendees
- You don't know what the mood of the group will be, or if there will be any active, willing participants or if people are going to give you fishy eyes when you start singing a chant

- You may never have seen the space or the ritual area before
- No time to set up any decorations
- Likely you only have a 45 minute time slot

I've shown up to events where the event organizers expected me to facilitate a ritual in an open end of the large and noisy vendor room. One ritual leader I met gets placed in a big noisy room for the annual Pagan Pride. She asked, "How can I do a ritual in a space like that and still make it good?"

The only answer I could really give her was, "Make it quick, make it loud. You won't have silence, you won't have people's attention span." Sadly, those are not great solutions.

So What Can You Do?
What you have control over is your ritual structure and your skills as a public speaker. These are the best tools you can leverage to get the group engaged. Get the group participating but in simple ways—a complicated logistic, or, a simple logistic that takes forever, is going to just drag the energy down. I frequently use a lot of chanting because I have the skill to get a group singing, though drumming can work too.

You may also be able to negotiate the ritual location. Talk to the organizers. At Festival of Souls in Memphis they always host their main ritual outside, however, it had been a really cold weekend, and I know that shivering people rarely can focus on the deep magic.

So I negotiated, we moved cleared out dinner tables to move the ritual to the main hall. It worked great. At Chicago Pagan Pride and at Pagan Picnic in St. Louis, the main ritual area is in an open area with no tree cover, however, there are shady areas to the side.

In both cases I've negotiated to move the ritual area over to where there is 1. Shade and 2. Trees for sound containment. It's a significant difference between a ritual where people are suffering in the sun and your voice is vanishing into nothing, and a ritual where people are reasonably more comfortable and people can hear you.

You can also bring people in closer. I've stood in a 150-person ritual circle in the hot sun. There were several ritual leaders, and I could only hear one of them. Bringing people closer so there are roughly concentric circles allows for an easier time projecting your voice.

What Doesn't Work
What won't ever achieve your goals is getting frustrated when your participants don't "get" what you're doing. I was at a ritual where one facilitator was trying to get a group of people singing a complicated chant. Out in the blazing sun, 150 people, and we could barely hear him. As he's going around trying to get us singing, he's visibly getting more and more frustrated and finally shouts at us, "Come on you guys, raise some energy!" If there's one phrase that will fail to raise energy, it's that.

The guy meant well, and I understand his frustration. However, the logistics of the heat and the huge circle worked against him, plus he was trying to engage the group in a complicated chant. Any activity you ask the group to participate in has to be 1. Skillfully facilitated and 2. Simple. If you're a really amazing facilitator and have a team, you can get people to do more complicated things, but that's Ritual Facilitation 501 level stuff.

Organizer Expectations
The more traveling and teaching that I do, the more it's important to clarify an organizer's expectations. The person working with you may not even realize they have specific assumptions. Some organizers work well via email, and some work better via phone. My own preference is email, as I'm a more visual person. I can usually tell when an organizer would be better to just get on the phone when I ask a bunch of questions and only perhaps one or two of those questions get answered. The organizer's not trying to be rude, they

probably are better verbal communicators. I won't go into learning modalities here but that's often the root of the communication disconnect.

I usually ask a few specific questions to get more information like, "Tell me a little about your festival culture. What types of things have people done at past rituals? Are there any traditions or expectations? Tell me a little about your group culture. Tell me a more about what type of ritual work you'd like to see, or what feedback you've had on rituals in the past."

Other questions can include logistics. "How many people usually attend the main ritual? What is the ritual area like, are there trees and shade, is it next to the road? Can we use fire?" You need to find out what you can do, and what you can't.

You need to know if they are expecting what I would call the "generic" ritual format of casting a circle, calling the four elements. I know of one Pagan Pride organizer that got upset at a group that hosted a ritual that was "nontraditional," ie, not Wicca-based. He hadn't thought to lay that out as an expectation, and they hadn't thought to ask.

In fact, that's one of the core challenges—most festival organizers, particularly for long-running festivals, are so used to their own festival culture that there's things they won't even think to mention. I remember one funny moment when I was working to plan the main ritual for Pagan Spirit Gathering in 2010 and we had the whole plan buttoned up until Nora Cedarwind Young said, "Oh, what about the Guardians!" and I asked, "Uh. What about the Guardians?" It turns out that the Guardians at PSG have a particular role in the main ritual every year. Failing to include them would have caused hurt feelings.

At a festival of the size and age of Pagan Spirit Gathering, there may be all sorts of traditions you aren't aware of, so the best thing you can do is ask.

Including Headliners and Other Leaders

You may be asked to include other leaders, clergy, or work in some of the headline presenters. When I'm folding in presenters or others I haven't worked with before, I try to approach this the way I'd like to be approached.

That is to say, if I'm ever at a festival and you need a helper for a ritual, I'm more than happy to step in and help you out for your ritual. But, don't expect me to just be able to walk in and do something really complicated. I can't lead five chants that you wrote and that I don't know.

So when I talk to a presenter at a Pagan event, I ask them if they'd like to be involved in the ritual and I also make clear that it's totally ok if they don't. If they are willing, I work with them to craft a ritual role that they and I are comfortable with. Some presenters are great ritualists. Some aren't. Some sing, others don't. My job is to make each person who takes a ritual role look good. For instance, if someone has a very quiet voice, they need a very short public speaking part.

There are any number of things in a festival ritual that you will have control over and that you won't have control over. Once you know what logistics you can work with, and which ones aren't available, and once you know what the expectations are, you can plan a ritual that will work for that particular scenario. The key is to ask a lot of questions up front, and be able to adapt to changes in the size of the group or deal with an unfavorable ritual spot.

Ritual: Physical Accessibility, Transgender Inclusion, and more

First published on www.PaganActivist.com

One of my values, as a Pagan leader, is to make rituals and spiritual experiences that are accessible and inclusive. At least--as much as I'm able to. I talk to a lot of Pagans who vehemently agree with this concept...and who then present rituals that--for various reasons--are not very accessible or inclusive.

Their rituals may present difficulty for people with mobility challenges. Or the rituals may not really be inclusive of gay, lesbian, or transgender community members. And there's lots of other ways rituals could be inaccessible and exclusive. Often this is done unintentionally; however, there is still an impact.

I've said before that activism is sometimes saying the unpopular thing. Often, it's standing up for those who do not have as much power in a dynamic, whose voices are not heard.

In this case, the unpopular thing is the idea that we--Pagan leaders and ritualists--may need to change how we approach rituals in order to make our rituals more accessible and inclusive. We may even need to re-evaluate some of our dearly-held theological beliefs. If we want the dominant culture to change, to legalize gay marriage, support people with disabilities, eliminate racism...don't we have to do that work first ourselves, within our community?

When I suggest making changes to rituals and "the way things are done," I've experienced some people have gotten pretty angry at me. A few months ago I posted a blog about the idea that Pagans shouldn't be using disposable cups for Cakes and Ale, and a number of Pagan ritualists and leaders said some harsh things in response. One of the overarching reactions I can sum up as, "It's too hard to do something different."
And let's face it--making changes to the way you've always done something is hard.

Usually my activism centers on environmentalism, but more and more within the Pagan community I find that we need activism on some basics...yes, environmentalism, but also, body image issues, health, positive sexuality, ethics. I observe that we don't always pay as much attention as we should to making space for people with different needs than our own.

Dogmatic Pagan Practices
I often hear Pagans wax poetic on how non-dogmatic we are. Modern Paganism is, in some ways, just as stuck in practices based in dogma as other religions. Ask any of these folks to look at a different way of doing things, and you might get an earful about how "this is the way we have always done it," or, "this is the way the gods want it done." If that's not dogma, then what is?

- In a group that has always used sage to smudge people, ask them to explore ways they might facilitate a ritual without any smoke
- In a group that expects everyone to stand through the whole ritual, ask them to think about ways to allow people to sit
- In a group who has always used the story of the God and Goddess and their heterosexual union for their wheel of the year, ask them to explore a story that is not solely based on gender binary or heterosexual sex
- In a group that has always had talking-heavy rituals, ask them to consider ways to include people with different learning modalities
- If I'm running a public ritual, it is my obligation to make space for as many people to be comfortable as possible.

Accessibility: Physical Mobility

Many Pagans have mobility challenges. Bad knees, fibromyalgia, back pain. For whatever reason, some people will have a hard time standing during rituals. An obligation I hold as a leader and ritualist is to make my rituals accessible to those with various physical needs. This includes everything from choosing a venue that is accessible to those with mobility challenges, to making sure that people in my ritual are empowered to sit.

I'm amazed at how many rituals go on and on, and people with canes who are in obvious discomfort will do their best to stand through a ritual. Most ritualists, I observe, never offer any physical accommodation for these folks.

A lot of accessibility can be managed by the ritualists and how much choice you offer your participants.

During my pre-ritual talk, I outline a few agreements such as, "I will be inviting people to stand, move, and sing, and if people need to sit down they are welcome to do so, that they can participate as much as they are physically able. If they need to bring a chair in closer they are welcome to do so, or to ask someone for help in doing so. "

If I'm hosting a spiral dance, I ask people who need to sit to come to the center so that they can participate seated. There are more ways to include people with mobility difficulties than I can outline here. But, because it's my value to make my ritual accessible, I don't see these accommodations as compromising my rituals.

Accessibility: Location, Transportation, Cost

Along the same lines, I work hard to make sure that my rituals are hosted close to public transportation and easy parking. I also work to find a venue that is inexpensive enough that I can offer my events on a sliding scale, with no one turned away for lack of funds. Achieving all of those goals inexpensively is no mean feat, which you probably know if you've ever organized a Pagan event.

Accessibility: Scent, Incense, Sage, and other Smoke

I've talked to many Pagans who are baffled when I suggest that I do not purify with sage. Some have even posed the question, "Is it even a real ritual without sage?" I personally facilitate almost all of my rituals without smoking/scented things. I, and many other Pagans, are allergic and sensitive to sage, incense, smoke, or other scents.

In fact, I get the question so often from ritual leaders who cannot conceive of how one might facilitate a ritual without incense, sage, or essential oils that I just published a short e-book on how to use scent appropriately, and how to facilitate potent rituals without using any scent, smoke, or fire. I personally would love to attend more rituals where I don't spend part or most of my time struggling to breathe.

Accessibility: Learning Modalities and Intelligences
Many Pagan rituals are very talky. In a way, they are similar to the classroom setting where teachers present most information as talking to students, with some visual support, and very little for kinesthetic learners. The idea of educational theory to work with multiple learning modalities and various intelligences is one that takes up more than just a blog post on its own.

In fact, facilitating for different learning modalities and intelligences is getting almost an entire chapter in the ritual book I'm writing. But one thing to consider is, are your rituals predominantly talky, thusly appealing to auditory learners? How do you include your visual learners, your kinesthetic learners, your emotional learners?

Do your rituals work to include both introverts and extroverts? Internal processors and external processors? Long processors and short processors?

While the theory of the Golden Rule--do unto others as you would have done to you--is a good one, the Golden Rule is occasionally a form of discrimination. When we assume that the experience of others is just like our own, we don't do a good job of planning and designing rituals that are accessible to people with other ways of being.

Tolerance, Intolerance, and GLBTQ Exclusivity
I hear a lot of Pagans talk about how Pagans are tolerant. Which seems to evaporate as soon as there's an opportunity to bash Christians on a

Facebook group, and doesn't seem to last very long when discussing different Pagan faiths either.

Tolerance also seems to last until someone suggests changing the way a group has always been run, or changing the way a ritual is done. It kind of comes across as, "I totally support gay marriage, but all my rituals are going to focus on heterosexual union between the Goddess and the God." In this article I wrote on gender inclusivity in rituals, I went far more in-depth into including transgender community members, as well as folks who prefer to work outside of the gender binary, as well as gay, lesbian, and bisexual community members.

As I said there, it's one thing to say, "GLBTQ folks are welcome here." It's another thing to choose stories that don't raise up the heterosexual union as the only divine life-cycle. Or to consciously choose language that is gender inclusive, chants that are inclusive. "When we say Goddess, we mean, the genderless divine," works about as well as saying that God in the Abrahamic traditions is genderless.

Theology and Inclusion

Most Pagan rituals I've been to lean pretty heavily on the gender binary. If a tradition is duotheistic--working with the God and the Goddess--then gender polarity and binary is a core part of that tradition's theology. Let's talk about the elephant in the room: How can rigidly duotheistic/bi-gendered tradition and rituals ever be inclusive of folks who don't work within the gender binary?

I'm not saying that if you're a duotheist you're wrong. In other articles I've talked about holding paradox when we communicate about things we disagree on. I can hold the paradox that you have the right to practice a duotheistic faith. However, I think the elephant is that we must acknowledge that a duotheistic faith may not appeal to transgender and non-gender-binary folks.

Similarly, if the core of your rituals centers on the heterosexual union of the God and Goddess, can you see how your gay and lesbian community members might not find that very inclusive? For that matter, I still hear debates among some BTW and other "old school" Wiccans along the lines of, "How can you properly initiate a priest/ess who is gay or lesbian, since the initiation only works when conferred (through sex or through ritualistic means) from a priest/ess of the opposite gender?"

I wonder if this is something that may shift over time. Not, "Your theology is wrong," but more that our understanding of gender today is far different from our understanding of gender when Wicca began rising in popularity in the mid 1900's. For that matter, coming out as gay or lesbian at that time was probably writing your own death warrant. Things have changed since then, and our theologies and dogmas may need to adapt in a way that most Abrahamic faiths have not been able to.

Similarly, I've written in past posts about the exclusion some Dianic groups participate in, barring entry to their rituals by any attendee who is a transgender woman and not a cisgender woman. Perhaps this, too, will ease in the decades to come when a transgender woman is just a woman. Or perhaps the popularity of one-gender-only groups will diminish as our population becomes more gender fluid.

What I know today is that I want to make my rituals inclusive of all genders and sexualities to the best of my ability, and that has meant changing how I do ritual, changing my language. I'm not an expert, but I do my best. My article linked above gives some insight into approaches I've taken, and I have more to learn.

Racial and Minority Inclusion
I'll admit, this is an area I struggle with. I'm white, I was raised in an all-white town where we were taught that the N-word is impolite, however, that you should lock your doors when you're in the city and there are black or brown people around.
When I first became Pagan, I never saw any Pagans of color, and I used to believe what I heard from other (white) Pagans. "Black people aren't really interested in Paganism." Or, "It's too Euro-Centric." "Black and Hispanic people have their own traditions, Voodoo and such." Consequently, at first I went under the (erroneous) assumption that any black Pagans I met were practicing African-Diasporic traditions like Vodou, which isn't necessarily the case.

Over time, I started seeing Pagans of color at events, but it was rare. My former partner was mixed-race, and I learned a lot while I was with him. I learned how alone and even afraid he felt when attending events; he would point out to me that he was almost always the only black guy in the room, and it was true. He was grateful beyond words when there was one other person of color at a Pagan event.

What I also noticed is that when he and I ran events together, more people of color attended.

As someone who is white, I'm not sure how to make my rituals more inclusive beyond the work I already do with open-language trance. Ie, instead of defining that the Goddess is blonde and has blue eyes, I let people determine what the divine looks like for themselves. If we're working with the story of a particular myth, such as the 9 Muses,

I'll point out that people can work with them as 9 female-gendered Greek deities, or, as 9 aspects of inspiration that go beyond gender or even a specific physical form...that each person is responsible for building up the imagery for how the divine looks to them.

Then again, I am a pantheist and an archetypist, not a hard polytheist, and it's not important to me that Greek deities look white, or that Egyptian deities look black. For me it's more about giving people the choice to shape the experience and their experience of the divine in whatever way works best for them.

I don't care what gender they see the divine as, what race, or even if the divine is human-shaped for them. Story and myth is powerful, and what's equally powerful is giving people to shape their own experience. I do this primarily through open-language trance--I ask people what they see, instead of telling them what the divine looks like for me. I hope to learn more about how I can better support making my events more accessible and inclusive for Pagans of color.

Feasibility and Cost

As a volunteer organizer, there's some accommodations I can't afford to make. Sometimes, I have to go with the cheaper venue. When I host a ritual in Chicago, I have one venue that I typically use that is on the ground floor and it's pretty accessible. But, it's not always available, and other venues are sometimes cheaper. One is up two flights of stairs.

Pagan festivals are often not physically accessible to everyone. People who have a difficulty walking or coping with the heat, people who need electricity to sleep with a CPAP machine, aren't necessarily going to be able to have their needs met, and there's only so much a festival organizer can do and make the festival viable.

If someone who is deaf attends one of my rituals, I have no budget to hire an interpreter, and I don't currently have access to a Pagan volunteer who can offer sign language. I have, perhaps three or four times, attended a few rituals where there was such a volunteer. I hope to find more people who could offer sign language for deaf participants.

It's difficult, as a Pagan event organizer, to take every single person's needs into account. Honestly, if I did, I'd never be able to offer an event. There's just no way to make an event that is inclusive of everyone. In fact, I wrote a blog recently about some of the challenges of planning Pagan events and some of the multitudes of wacky complaints I get.

Exclusive: When it's OK
There are times when I consciously make the choice to create a ritual that may be exclusive. If I'm facilitating a ritual that is an intense ordeal and includes fasting and physical hardship, that's not a ritual that's for everyone.

If I chose to offer a healing ritual for women who have had miscarriages or abortions, or if I offered a healing ritual for families (all genders) who have had to cope with the same. Either one of those is exclusive, and for a particular purpose.

Sometimes it's also appropriate to kick someone out of a ritual for bad behavior. Perhaps their bad behavior is because of a learning disability or a mood disorder. But, if someone's being consistently disruptive or even aggressive, then I may need to bar them from events.

I've worked to accommodate many people over the years; folks with Aspergers, with a personality-altering brain injury, Narcissists, Borderlines, Bipolar, people on medication for anger management. Ultimately, I'm willing to work with people, but if they become consistently harmful to the group, my responsibility is ultimately to the larger group.

Commitment
My commitment is to try and make accommodations where I can. I do my best, and it's not always enough. Sometimes it's a matter of finances; I dream of the day when Pagan events and groups bring in enough money so that I don't have to make the impossibly hard choice between an accessible and non-accessible venue. Sometimes it's a matter of volunteers; I also dream of the day when I have people to offer services such as signing during rituals or workshops, or people to coordinate children's programming at events.

Sometimes, it's a matter of taking on a learning curve. I'm white, cisgender, and predominantly heterosexual. I'm pretty physically strong. I'm not an expert in transgender inclusion. I'm not gay or lesbian. I'm not a minority. I don't contend with a major physical disability.

However, I have compassion. I don't know what it's like to be beaten for being gay, don't know what it's like to suffer systemic racial discrimination. I do know what it's like to be rejected, abused, and harmed for other things. My experiences aren't the same--but they help me to have some context for what others face. It is through that compassion that I work to make space for people to attend ritual and spiritual work, to find a home in community.

And sometimes, it means standing up to call our Pagan community and leaders out for policies that are, intentionally or unintentionally, exclusive and discriminatory.
How can we work to learn how to make our rituals more accessible and inclusive? Will you commit to work to help more Pagans find Home?

Confidence in Facilitation: Using the Magical Feather

First published in CIRCLE Magazine Issue 102

I remember the first rituals I attended, watching the priests and priestesses in the center facilitating invocations and deeper work, addressing the group clearly and confidently. I remember thinking, "I could never do that."

Later, I felt the strong call to leadership in my spiritual tradition. Eventually I learned how to facilitate rituals, workshops, and grow comfortable speaking in front of others. A lot of what I needed to go from stage fright into ritual facilitation was tool that works a lot like the Magic Feather that Dumbo the elephant is given. Dumbo is given this feather and told that as long as he has it, he can fly.

I also learned, through this process, how to empower others in stepping into new roles. As a leader, I have the tendency many leaders share of being a control freak, so making space for others to step into new skill-sets is some of the most agonizing leadership work that I do. And, some of the most rewarding. The Magic Feather is a tool you can use to empower your group members and make your team, and your group's work, stronger.

Shy Beginnings

Have you ever been to afraid to speak in public? Do you work with people who are afraid to take ritual roles? When I began stepping into Pagan leadership, I thought, surely I can do this without public speaking; I can take out the trash, do dishes—these are spiritual acts in an earth-based tradition.

I joined the Diana's Grove Mystery School program to progress through their training program for leaders in alternative spirituality. Their model is based on servant leadership—that leaders are there to serve the group, and that this often means the strongest leaders may not be in the center facilitating; they might be doing grunt work behind the scenes. This sounded perfect to me; I liked doing grunt work, and was afraid to speak in front of groups.

However, Diana's Grove used a fairly sneaky Magic Feather with me in their program.
Diana's Grove hosted monthly retreats offering personal growth work, community building, and leadership training. Their philosophies valued inclusion, and they encouraged all participants to join an exercise called Community Created Invocations that would happen during the rituals amongst the weekend's events.

Participants are intentionally set up for success in this—the elemental invocations were facilitated by a staff member, and supported by members of the leadership program. While the overall ritual was planned by several staffers in the morning, the Community Created Invocations provided an opportunity for everyone there to help plan a small piece of the ritual, and to step in as much as they are comfortable.

In this case, the Magic Feather was offered to each of us doing the invocations. Each participant had a safety net: the choice of how much to be involved, the safety of the Diana's Grove community, and the support of the staff. Still, I was nervous, and initially I supported more nonverbally with body-motion. Later I progressed on to speaking. I knew that there were other nervous people in the group with me, so I didn't feel alone. And I knew that all the staffers were there to support me. If I asked them to take a breath with me to call in Air, they would breathe in wholeheartedly. I became more comfortable with ritual work and being seen; I became more comfortable with taking that risk.

As I moved into the Diana's Grove leadership program, I was given progressively more visible ritual roles. Sometimes my heart would still pound before stepping in, but the staff never asked me to do anything I was not ready for, and they would offer me mentoring in preparation for doing something new.

Empowering Others
As a leader of a group, one of your roles may be to empower new members of the circle to step into roles of increasing visibility.
I found myself in the position of the leader of a group of Diana's Grove participants living in St. Louis. There, I found myself needing to offer the Magic Feather to some members of my team as they stepped into facilitation roles. The St. Louis Mysteries group offered public rituals, monthly workshops, and daylong Pagan conferences. With such activities, everyone on the team needed to increase their skills as leaders, myself included.

As a servant of my leadership team, I worked to create opportunities for them to become stronger leaders. Some of the team were as deathly afraid of speaking as I had been, and yet I knew they had it in them.

As I began to facilitate the process of empowering my team members, I realized how tricky this was.

The Magic Feather, like any tool of air, is a delicate art. I often felt like the Egyptian scale of Ma'at where the heart is weighed against a feather.

On the one hand, as a facilitator of public events, it is my job to serve community and offer an excellent experience to the participants. On the other hand, as a leader, I also feel it's my job to facilitate inclusivity and empower group members to step into more challenging roles.

Excellence, or inclusivity? How would I keep them in balance?

Tools for Success: Belief
As many times as I've sat in the "hot seat" watching someone new and unskilled take on a ritual role, I find that the stress is personally and professionally worth it. I remember the day a woman facilitated a small philosophy piece for the first time and did a fine job. She was clearly nervous. However, supporting that piece broke her through her fears, and she stepped into more facilitation work and leadership roles. Offering her the support that she needed at that event helped her find her voice as a facilitator. She just needed someone to support her, and tell her, "You can do it."

I find that a lot of the Magic Feather is being a cheerleader for the team members; relentlessly supporting the team, and offering my confidence that they could do things. At the core, the Magic Feather is about belief—when my team didn't believe in themselves, I offered them the Feather of my belief in them.

Structure of Support
There are other tools that are part of the Feather. It takes a strong leader to be able to hold together the kind of structure that can handle new people taking roles. Some skills include the ability to see and hold a large vision, patience, and good communication.
I find it also helps to have good supporting structure. My mentors at Diana's Grove had set me up for success in a number of ways that ensured excellent events, and inclusion of new facilitators, with co-facilitated ritual. The St. Louis Mysteries group offered a monthly gathering in the format of a co-facilitated workshop with a ritual.

These gatherings proved to be a fantastic format to give people manageable pieces of facilitation.

Give people roles that they can handle: Break down roles into smaller pieces if needed, or pair people up with a stronger team member.

Start with a strong plan: The St. Louis Mysteries gatherings were planned by either a few people who distributed the plan and roles, or co-created by the whole team, but in both cases the plans were guided by the people with the most experience.

Communicate expectations: The plans were sent to the team via email, which gave people a chance to ask questions and get more information. Before the event, the team would run through the ritual plan, and any final questions could be answered. Reviewing the plan with the whole team helps everyone to see how each piece feeds into the next.

Lead strong and set the tone: The first five minutes of a ritual or class sets the energetic tone for the whole event. Within the plan, I always ensure that strong facilitator speaks before a weaker facilitator. This energetically warms up the room.

Actively support: As the event is going on, I and the other team members, are actively engaged and supporting the person who is facilitating. For me, this is being fully present to their offering, and being on hand in case the facilitator stumbles to help them out, or to handle a challenging participant. I'm also making mental notes of how they did.

Cheerlead: Remind the team that you believe in them, and that we're all in this together, supporting one another.

Tools of Air: The Magic Feather
Here's an elemental process working with the tool of Air and

communication for how to offer just the right Magic Feather to an emerging facilitator.

Earth: Listening and Observing—What are the gifts of your team? Where do they need work? What do they want out of this? I watched the members of my leadership team, learned what their skills and talents were, and where their edges were. I asked them what they wanted as leaders and facilitators, and listened to their answers.

Air: Thinking and Analyzing—I processed what I'd observed, and thought about what facilitation opportunities would ensure success for each individual. Which edges could I push? When was I risking the excellence of the event? What challenging work would support their process?

Fire: Speaking—I communicate with the person about the role I'd like them to take. What are the expectations of the role? I set my team member up well when I provide them with a strong plan with clear expectations of what was expected of them. Usually I would focus on the intention of the piece, not necessarily the logistics of how it's to be done, unless the person needed me to talk through or model what logistics might support their piece.

Water: Compassionate Feedback—offer positive feedback immediately after the workshop, let the team member know what they did well. Let them know that they fulfilled the intention of the piece. This isn't the time to tell them they were visibly nervous, stuttered, forgot something, and went over time. This is perhaps the hardest part of the Feather—being a cheerleader can be more important than giving technically correct feedback.

More specific feedback can be given at the feedback session. Always indicate what they did well, and initially, keep any constructive feedback to a minimum. The point here is to give them confidence. If someone really screwed something up, that feedback should be given in private, but remember to look at the whole event. If someone stumbled over their words, did it ruin the whole event? Probably not. In a situation where the person knew she was visibly nervous, I told her, "I could tell you were a little nervous, but the conversation about that philosophy point was engaging, and your facilitation got people talking about that point and engaged in the work. Good job."

Feedback Tips
I highly recommend the tools of Non-Violent Communication for feedback. Good feedback references what the person did, not the person themselves. Many people hear feedback such as, "I didn't find your invocation powerful," as, "You really suck," depending on their self-esteem. I try to be transparent about what I'm giving feedback on, and as non-shaming as possible. I don't judge them or make assumptions for what they were feeling.

Feedback seems to get across the best when I reference the physical reality of what they have done, and the impact that it had on me, and the impact I perceived it had on the group. I also try to not present the feedback with a fake smile—people see right through that.

My best feedback is offered in a voice that's not emotionally charged, and I'll point out something like, "You definitely met the intention of the piece, but I had a hard time following your concept at one point. I also noticed that your body language didn't convey to me what you were talking about, and I think stronger body language would have made the piece more powerful." This feedback doesn't judge them, just indicates some places that needed work.

Instead of trying to tell the person the thousand things they did wrong, I recommend writing these things down, and work up a training session to address facilitation deficiencies instead of bringing them up as feedback that could destroy the person's confidence. It can work to offer a workshop yourself, or bring in someone from outside the group.

A few times I failed to properly set facilitators up for success, and they really struggled with a piece. If the piece is short, I found the least shaming option was to let the person finish their piece without intervention, even if they are flubbing the concept. A few minutes of poor facilitation won't kill anyone in the group. In very few cases I've stepped in to transition things to something else.

Before giving feedback, think about your own intentions, and the nature of your role as a leader. If your intention is for someone to become a strong facilitator and strong leader on the team, it makes sense to offer them the cheerleading that is the root of the Magic Feather. The magic of this is the confidence it inspires.

The magic of this Feather is when a person begins to believe in themselves, and suddenly the talented facilitator within them feels comfortable emerging. Every time I told someone they did a good job, they believed it, and did a better job next time. Did they do a perfect job? Of course not, but by giving them an opportunity to try out their wings, they eventually learned to fly.

Flying Without the Feather
As people became more skilled in their facilitation, I faced another question—When was it time to take away the feather? Each person will have different needs.
There's usually a point when it makes sense to give someone more specific feedback about what they have done if they are going to grow. This point is usually when they have developed a measure of personal confidence; sometimes they will ask for more specific feedback.

Specific constructive feedback is an act of generosity. If someone on my team wants to step into larger ritual roles, I owe it to them to offer them feedback so that they can grow in skill. If I'm withholding feedback, I'm withholding a gift that they need to take them to that next level. As students and team members become peers, they no longer need the Feather.

Set Up for Success
Of course, the Feather in and of itself doesn't hold any special properties—the magic of the Feather is that the new facilitators are putting their faith in you, as a leader, and your belief in them. Eventually, they'll begin to believe in themselves, and the Magic Feather becomes what it always was, a catalyst for their own personal magic and talents.

I still remember the first ritual role I held at Diana's Grove that took me deeper into the ritual instead of over analyzing what I had done. That fire invocation took me deeper into the theme. I remember looking into someone's eyes as I held a torch to bring the fire of the Seeker into the circle. I could see the impact the invocation had on him—how he, too, felt the call of that fire, how he reached for it. I felt the call of the fire in myself, and I was transformed by that sensation.

How can you offer your team members this Magic Feather? When have you held onto a Feather someone gave you?

Section Four: Safety, Ethics, and Healing in Rituals

Safety and Ethics in Rituals and Groups

First published in Crow Calls

Imagine both the best, and the worst, rituals you've ever been to—or even facilitated. What makes some rituals good? What makes them bad? For many participants, an intense, deeply emotional and spiritually transformative experience is what marks the best rituals. However, when a ritual is unsafe, the very intensity and emotion of a transformative ritual can be what makes it a negative experience.

It is, however, certainly possible to have potent rituals that uphold safety for participants. Similarly, when organizing any small spiritual or grass roots group, many of these tools can be used to ensure a safe and ethical environment.

What are your Values?

Different groups, leaders, and ritualists will have different approaches and values around safety and ethics. The definition of ethics is "A system of moral principles: the ethics of a culture" or " the moral principles, as of an individual," or "that branch of philosophy dealing with values relating to human conduct, with respect to the rightness and wrongness of certain actions and to the goodness and badness of the motives and ends of such actions."

Thusly, the first step in establishing safety is to explore your spiritual tradition, and what your values are around safety. After that, establishing a set of agreements for the group—and upholding them—offers continuity and stability. Communicating these agreements to any potential ritual participants or group members ensures that everyone is on the same page. When transparent communication of agreements is not present, that leads to unclear assumptions and expectations. This almost invariably leads to disappointment, if not fear, anger, or betrayal.

For example, can you imagine attending a ritual at an event that is listed as: "Opening ritual: This ritual will open the day and celebrate the season," and then arriving to find yourself engaged in a ritual lasting an hour and a half with an intensive journey into the Underworld and a physical ordeal in the middle? It's critical to set up expectations. There's usually nothing wrong with a journey to the Underworld, but people generally appreciate a heads up so that they can choose whether or not to attend a ritual like that.

Spectrum of Mercy to Severity
If I look at ritual safety along a spectrum using the Kabbalistic pillars of Mercy and Severity, on one end I have Mercy. My rituals will be on this end if I highly value a harmless, careful, and secure experience. Rituals on this end of the spectrum won't use any sage for fear someone might be allergic, won't use any language that might challenge someone, and are going to be focused on non-threatening topics. Likely rituals on this side of the spectrum are primarily celebratory and don't push for a lot of intimacy, intensity, or edge. Intensity and depth is sacrificed for structure, harmony, order, predictability.

On the side of Severity, these rituals are on the edge of the edge. Physical ordeals, transformative experiences without any boundaries, shamanic initiations that can lead to insanity or death. Safety is sacrificed for intensity.

Most rituals will sit somewhere in between these two poles. For myself, I find that the most effective rituals straddle the gray area effectively, using both Mercy and Severity as needed. The rituals I'm facilitating usually have a transformative and personal growth component. They also use ecstatic and shamanic techniques that, depending on the ritual, may use a lot of energy and emotional intensity to effect the transformation.

However, I have found that I can often do deeper and more transformational work by ensuring that some basic needs for safety and structure are met. By holding a strong "container," seeing to people's comforts and ensuring people have information about what's going on, participants are more willing to dive deep than they would be if we offered a more overtly intimidating, "Severity" type of ritual.

For most rituals, I would say that the depth participants are willing to go is very much related to the safety of the container. I look at the blending of mercy and severity as the spiritual version of, "I'm going to set your bone, and it's going to hurt like heck, but I'm doing it out of love and compassion and making sure you trust me enough to do this."

There are several progressive categories of safety, including physical comfort, information, and emotional safety. If I am planning a ritual with a fair amount of intensity and emotional/personal transformation, to be successful at this I'll need to set up safeties in all of those areas before a participant is willing to trust me enough to go to the dark places within.

Physical comfort
Several of my mentors used to tell me that it's practically impossible to think about personal growth when we're outside and shivering in

the cold. With a few exceptions, I think they're right on. Whenever there are physical distractions—too hot, too cold, too many bugs, a bad smell, a loud sound—people's ability to focus on the work at hand will be reduced.

I look at establishing a physically safe place as both a tool to build a stable container, as well as common courtesy for the attendees. Look at all the physical needs people may have, from basics to more advanced things. Is there a comfortable bathroom? Do people have access to drinkable water, to food, to a place to sit down? If it's hot, is there shade? If it's cold, is there heat, or blankets? Are accommodations available for participants with injuries or mobility challenges?

For some rituals, it may be appropriate to engage in a physical ordeal, such as fasting, a sweat lodge, sleep deprivation, or something else. If there is a physical component, such as movement exercises, it's not always necessary to "dumb down" your work for people with less physical ability, though it is important to communicate if your participants are expected to be up at 7am doing Yoga for 3 hours, and also expected to continue movement exercises and chanting while in 105 degree heat. Some workshops and rituals require an intensive physical discipline, which is fine if participants have agreed to do this. Sweat lodges, martial arts, flesh pulls, vision quests with fasts, are all examples of physical challenges that might be part of a ritual, and for obvious reasons should be communicated well beforehand.

And yes, I've heard of ritual leaders who were planning to ask participants to engage in body modification on the spot with no warning. While it's true that sometimes you may want an element of surprise to some of the challenges in your rituals, particularly intensive ordeal rituals, there's a huge gulf between a surprise and something that is physically dangerous.

Physical Ability

On a less intensive scale, even when doing something like a Spiral Dance or having participants stand up to approach someone at an altar, it's important to note if anyone in the circle cannot walk and might need a different way to physically engage. For Spiral Dance, you can place people in chairs at the center facing out, for instance. If other participants are going to multiple altars, someone might need assistance doing that, or, might need the people from those altars to come to them.

It's also important to minimize physical distractions—phones going off in ritual, packs of dogs running through the middle of the ritual, etc.

Having a trained fire tender or other people managing those kinds of physical safeties is important. At one gathering, there were amazing fire tenders and a large camp fire that was lit throughout the gathering. During an alchemical ritual, we were engaging in the Calcination phase of the alchemical process where we burn away the old stories that no serve us. I had a decanter of rubbing alcohol to create a flash effect in the fire. I misjudged the amount of alcohol to drop onto the fire and the fire flared up fairly high. Something like this, if anyone had been too close to the fire, could absolutely kill your efforts to make the group feel safe!

Ritual theatrics are also an important tool set and can assist in creating the atmosphere for intensive work, but mistakes in with fire effects are easy to make. If you, like me, use these techniques, it's worth the effort to learn how to do them safely and effectively.

Information

There's a balance between total secrecy and surprises, and too much information. Imagine attending a week-long intensive after you've just had knee surgery, and finding out on-site that it's a requirement to hike a mile with all attendees every morning. Imagine attending a ritual for Samhain and realizing in the middle of the ritual that a priestess was going to be aspecting/drawing down Persephone, and individually and publicly confronting each person with their deepest wounds.

Here is where a little information can give people what they need without giving away too much of the inner mysteries of the ritual. I find that offering enough information up front not only ensures people know what is going on, but it also will engage and enthuse participants for the specific kind of ritual that is being offered.

Information can also address physical comforts, like letting people know where the bathrooms are, how they can get access to water, and letting people know that it's all right to bring their chairs closer to the fire to get warm. If there are any specific agreements your groups or ritual has, communicating some of these can help participants who are unsure how to engage.

Some information I'm willing to let stay as an assumption—I assume that my participants aren't going to just start punching one another, for instance. But if I'm taking participants into a ritual of deep personal transformation where they release an old wound and I know that some people will cry, I offer the agreement of self responsibility—that each person should take care of their own physical needs, as well as their emotional needs. That if they need assistance they can ask for it, and if they are going through an emotional process like crying or screaming, I'm going to assume they are doing what they need to do and I'm not going to interrupt that process or over-tend people. Yet, I'll also make sure that people know if they get stuck in a bad place emotionally, that they can call on me or other ritual leaders for support.

Emotional Safety
Having your basic physical needs met, and having enough information, will allow me as a participant to feel more emotionally safe. Most rituals use various techniques to engage both facilitators and participants in an altered state of consciousness, or trance state,

which is what allows us to seek in the depths and transform. Some emotional safety in a group comes from intimacy—from knowing who is there, knowing how much it's safe to open up.

Some of this comes from trust of the facilitator. Before I begin a ritual, I take some time to outline what will be going on in the ritual, and establish my credibility. Later, when participants are in an altered state, they will be willing to go with me into the Underworld because they can trust that I will bring them back.

One of the ways I offer participants a way to go deep in a way that feels safer for them is that I'm going to be vulnerable first. I don't ask people to go where I won't go first. So if I'm asking people to make a sound of grief or rage, I (or other co-facilitators) make the sound first to make it safe for others to go to that place. I also first offer the safeties of information around what happens when we have emotions in ritual, so that one person who starts to cry doesn't freak someone else out who wasn't expecting that.

Often the way I approach intensity in ritual is through depth of emotion and vulnerability. If I'm going to facilitate a ritual that could take people to a dark place, I'm going to ensure that I have people in a role as "safeties" to keep an eye on the folks who are having the biggest emotional responses. I want to ensure that participants aren't fussed over, because that offers an entirely separate dynamic where the participant is rewarded (by attention) for being dramatic or hysterical. However, I also want to be sure there are enough folks present who can help someone ground, or talk and process, if they went a little too deep.

Unethical Facilitation
Within the realm of transformative rituals, it is possible to facilitate in a way that crosses into the territory of unethical. Here are some red flags:

Facilitator is pressuring you to do things you aren't comfortable doing. There's a difference between "I feel you're on the edge of something important, are you willing to push just a little past your current edge?" and, "You are not a real practitioner if you won't do this."

It's all about me. If the ritualist seems to be doing things in order to be in the spotlight and get the group to look at them, or they do flashy things in ritual instead of empowering others to take roles.

Intensity for its own sake. Intensity is a potent tool when used for a purpose, but when a ritualist seems to be upping the ante all the time and driving the group into further intensity, it's time to ask why, particularly if they are pressuring people into physically challenging or even physically harmful situations.

Cult leader/power trip. Some of the above are factors in the cult leader scenario. Other factors might include manipulating group members, mood swings that leave participants feeling on thin ice all the time but yet feeling like they have to support the leader, otherwise known as codependence. If the facilitator is stroking their own ego at the expense of the ritual or the group, that's a red flag.

Sexually inappropriate. If you're being pressured to take off your clothes or engaged in sex acts, and you didn't sign on for a sex temple, it's time to get out.

Physical danger. Here the facilitator puts the group into physical danger, or engages in a violent act that scares people. This might involve harming someone as part of a ritual. As mentioned above, there's a place for ordeal rituals like flesh pulls, but if the violence is unexpected, if the physical danger is intended to make the facilitator look cool or edgy, or if the physical danger is a result of the facilitator pressuring people, that's where it becomes dangerous.

Creepy. If things generally feel creepy, try to look at what is physically or emotionally being asked of you, follow your gut feeling.

Measuring Success

I can often judge how well a ritual has gone by how people are acting at the end. When I'm facilitating public rituals in Chicago, when folks are hanging out 2-3 hours after the ritual, long after the potluck table has been denuded of its bounty, the ritual probably went well. On the other hand, if people scatter quickly, or if someone's melting down for 2 hours after the ritual, or if people generally feel uncomfortable long after the event, I may not have set up appropriate safeties.

One part of safety is having a process of feedback. When participants know that you value what their experience was, this shows them that you are there in service, not in ego. It's also a good practice to grow your skills as a ritualist and leader.

While the focus of this article is about rituals, many of these are tools that can be applied to leadership of groups as well.

Thoughts on Ritual, Psychology, and Therapy

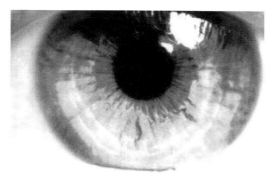

On various online forums in the holistic, alternative spirituality, Earth-centered, and Pagan communities, I've seen people make the bold statement that ritual and magic should take the place of psychotherapy. In fact, I've seen people actively discourage people from seeking therapy, referring to therapy as useless or even harmful for those with non-mainstream spiritual beliefs.

I don't agree with that perspective at all.

The question to ask is, what do we want out of our lives? Do we want to live better, healthier lives? If so, then the next question is, how do we get there? And how can we encourage practices that help each of us to live our fullest potential? I believe that ritual work as well as psychological techniques such as therapy can both work together help us get there.

In fact, I have benefited greatly from therapy and from practices and personal work that come from psychotherapy and psychology. I believe that those of us who choose the path of holistic healing, alternative spirituality, or even just being "spiritual but not religious," can still get a lot out of therapy. As I sometimes say, "Magic can't fix everything."

But, we can also get a lot out of various holistic practices too. Reiki, sound healing, meditation, and other rituals or ceremonies. It doesn't have to be either or. It's possible that both of these tools can work to inspire health and wellness, particularly for our minds and souls.

Baby and the Bathwater
I believe that the field of psychology generally threw out the baby with the bathwater and divorced spirit from the mind. A a lot of psychotherapy doesn't fulfill our deep needs for ritual, among other things. However, there are psychologists and psychology schools working to bring the baby back into the bathwater. Carl Jung did rather a lot on that front, though there's still more work to do.

At the same time, a lot of folks in the new age, Pagan , and alt spiritual community want to rely on energy healing and ritual when that isn't enough. For some of the psychological and psychiatric issues some people are facing, ritual is not enough. Ritual work might help someone going through a crisis, but that person needs long-term counseling as well. A ritual or spell or Reiki healing isn't going to suddenly fix someone struggling with Bipolar.

The problem is that in the alternative spirituality community, we have a lot of skills with complementary healing techniques, however, we don't have the professional skills in most of our ad-hoc groups for things like pastoral counseling, much less for in-depth psychotherapy. And that's not even touching the whole aspect of people who need meds to balance their brain chemistry. When I hear people say that therapy is useless, or even dangerous, that's throwing out the baby with the bathwater too.

"There was this one person…"

Now—some of the arguments against therapy are perhaps valid. I've heard horror stories of people who tried to explain their experiences of empathy, spirit communication, work with different deities, psychic abilities, or other alternative spiritual practices to their therapist. I've heard of folks who were met with everything from chiding and derision to being diagnosed with various disorders, and all because they were honest about their own spirituality.

However, I feel compelled to note here that most of these horror stories are anecdotal, and are told second and third hand. What I mean is, I've never actually talked to anyone who has had this experience. It's always, "I heard about this one girl who..." stories. I think that a little fear goes a long way. It's not to say that this doesn't happen. Anyone practicing a minority spirituality or lifestyle should feel out a therapist before hiring them.

I know of several people engaging in an ethical polyamorous lifestyle, for instance, who have been chastised and even threatened by their therapists or doctors. You know what's right for you, and if you're working with a medical professional who is judging you for an alternative lifestyle, it's time to hire someone else.

Why is Therapy Important?
One of the things people will hear me say a lot when I teach leadership and personal growth is, go get therapy. There's a ton of issues that come up when we're exploring ourselves. When I do a workshop on "Finding your Personal Magic," or a shadow-work ritual where we face our shadows, or a leadership class where we discuss our own issues as leaders, things come up. We realize, we have an ego, and maybe we have some problems with egotism that are getting in the way of being a better leader.

Or maybe we have terrible self esteem. Or maybe we are so afraid of naming the thing we want for our lives, our big dream, that we can't even speak it, can't even articulate that we have magic, that we have power. Or maybe we're terrified of public speaking. Or maybe we're terrible enablers and codependents and people pleasers. Or maybe we're high-strung Type-A and we drive away our volunteers.

What therapy helped me with was having a sounding board. To get outside of my head. While I wish I could have afforded therapy for longer–because, therapy definitely is a process that requires building a rapport with a therapist who knows you–I was able to get an outside perspective for some of the hamsterwheeling I was doing. I was also able to help pin down some of why I got as depressed as I do. I have a lot of avoidance behaviors; when I have screwed something up like missed a deadline when something was due, I bury my head in the sand and avoid calls or emails, and I spiral into depression. A lot of tools from Cognitive Behavioral Therapy helped me get out of the mythic mindset and out of that downward spiral. It's not 100%, but I'm way better than I used to be.

In fact, I can't even articulate all the ways that psychology and therapy has helped me. There's no way I would be able to do the public speaking I regularly do, or face my social anxiety, or lead groups, without the therapeutic work I've done.

Skill-building
One of the reasons that I say that alternative spirituality shouldn't throw therapy out is that there are very, very few leaders in the Pagan and alternative spirituality communities that have the skills to facilitate rituals and ceremonies and other healing work that can completely take the place of therapy. There are, for instance, a number of Pagans who have gained the skills to be pastoral counselors, and more Pagans beginning to work toward getting a Masters of Divinity or in general attending Pagan seminary classes to build those skills. There are Pagan leaders with a background in psychology.

My mentors had that background, and it's a big part of why their work was so effective.
Therapy and ritual can work in concert. We'd be foolish, as ritual leaders and professionals, to discard the amazing tools discovered within the art and science of psychology, especially tools within

Jungian/depth psychology which are a beautiful crossover to mythology and ritual work.

The original therapists were shamans, the medicine workers/healers/spirit communicators. Many of the techniques pioneered by modern psychology actually were originally practiced by the community healer. But, when the tools are taken out of context and spirit is divorced from mind, something is lost. However, that something that was lost is exactly what we find in ritual and spiritual work that focuses on personal transformation.

To increase my own skill sets in this area, I read articles and books on psychology. I learn about the neuroscience and trance states. I've even thought about going back to school to get more formal education in this area. There's a MA in Transformative Leadership and Transformative Arts that I've been dying to do for years. In the mean time, I continue to learn as much as I can. I network with therapists in the Pagan, shamanic, and holistic communities and pick their brains whenever I can.

Transformative Ritual
The types of rituals I host are psychologically intensive. They ask people to release what no longer serves, to face their shadows, in order to reach for our dreams, our destiny, our vision of who we could be. That's tough work. And, while the rituals I offer are a tremendous catalyst for people seeking that work, they aren't the whole process. They can crack open the shell, but therapy or counseling is a place where individuals can take the work further, where people can break out of old patterns.

When people find that moment of catharsis in a ritual or workshop, that's when I encourage them to try therapy or counseling. It's not a bad thing, it's not a judgment saying, "You're nuts and need help." It's saying, if you want to take responsibility for your spiritual growth and your personal work, this is a way that you can get some assistance in doing that.

Beyond ritual work, many people will need a long-term therapeutic/counseling process. I believe that something like this can be offered by a spiritual leader in an alternative spiritual tradition, provided that minister, priest, priestess, shaman, Druid, or guru has at least some training as a pastoral counselor. However, there are some things that it really helps to have help from someone who has more extensive training. Pastoral counseling is often bridging the gap to get someone to a deeper process of therapy. Some folks just need someone to talk to about their spiritual process, they just need someone to listen to them. Some people have never really had that—ever—in their lives. A person to just listen to them. And that's a lot of what pastoral counseling is, just listening.

But there's also a point when I recognize that someone is above my pay grade. That, I can listen to them, but they need more in-depth help than I can offer. And it's not a bad thing at all. Therapy is an opportunity for us to face those old bad habits and work to course correct so that we're engaging in life in a way that's fulfilling. What do You Want?

I believe that the marriage between psychology and spiritual work with rituals and rites of passage will bear some amazing fruit in the coming years. But to get there, those of us in alternative spiritual leadership have to learn many of the skills that we have lost. And, we have to work with the field of psychology that has thrown out a lot of the baby with the bathwater. There's a place where these overlap and meet. Where psychology informs ritual work. Where both work together so that we can be who we want to be.

Who would you be if you didn't have the pain of your past holding you back? If you didn't engage in the self-destructive patterns that keep you from the things you'd like to do? I work every day to live a life of joy. I don't always get there, but through both transformative ritual work as well as therapy, I'm closer along the path than I was before doing that work.

RITUAL FACILITATION

Healing From our Past

First published in the Edge Magazine October 2013

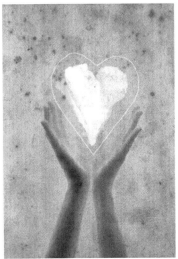

I facilitate extemporaneous, ecstatic, inclusive ritual that lends itself very well to personal transformation and the healing of old emotional wounds. These rituals are focused on personal work, on becoming our most excellent selves, reaching for our inner divine.

In reaching for that something larger, there is our broken hearts, the wounds of our past, the shadows that dog our steps. There are the obstacles that stand in our way, the barriers that keep us from becoming more, from reaching for our dreams. There is the pain of what's been done to us, and what we've done in turn.

Sometimes I think the hardest part of the process of healing is that moment when we wake up and realize that we are so often our own worst enemy. That, even though it may have been others that hurt us, that we keep those old wounds, old stories, alive and thriving in our own lives.

I believe there are many components to effective energy healing, but here are three.

Sound and Music Healing
I believe that the magic of movement and sound, of singing and toning and drumming and making rhythm together, is another core component. Sound, on its own, is a powerful agent of shifting our

energy, of healing. Sometimes sound--the right sound--can intensify energy. Gong bath, the right chant, the right harmonics, can absolutely intensify the healing energy.

Take Responsibility for our Own Healing
Some of the magic of ecstatic ritual and of healing is forgiving ourselves. Opening to a possibility of healing, and being willing to reach for it. For that matter, taking responsibility for the process of our own healing. While many of the techniques I use in rituals are similar to many shamanic traditions of soul retrieval, for me it's important to not do the journeying work for the participants in the ritual, but more, to facilitate their own journey of healing.

I don't believe that energy healing works as a prescription or recipe. Light this candle, sing this song,. Nor do I believe that energy healing works in the way some people define magic as "something that I don't have to do any work to get." Energy healing sets the intention, but we have to do the hard work of changing our own stories.

Changing our Selves, changing our stories of our Selves, is hard work. Whether that's our story that we can't stop smoking, or our story that we can't eat healthy, or our story that nobody likes us because all the kids in grade school made fun of us...whatever our story is, we are the ones who can change it.

Active Participation
Energy healing doesn't work when we don't participate. So often I hear from people who want to know what color candle to burn, or, want me to sing a healing song for them. They want me to do it for them, but the truth is, only we can heal ourselves.

With energetic healing, that means we need to participate in building that energy. In the ecstatic rituals I facilitate, I work to help people sing, chant, drum, dance, move, and use emotional intensity and intention in order to focus energy for transformation and healing. I believe that an actual emotional connection to that intention of healing is the most important of these, but being willing to move and sing and add energy through participation is key.

We ourselves are potent energy batteries. There's an amazing documentary, "Dances of Ecstasy," where an African healer articulates it brilliantly. They must have asked him, "Why do you dance in order to heal?" He responds very matter-of-factly and says something about how without the dancing, there is no energy to do the healing. I've read in a number of places that shamanic work is about spiritual heat. We raise up that spiritual heat, whether through intense dancing, or through rocking back and forth through the song of shared grief.

I often say that, in a ritual, I'm not there to heal you, I'm there to help you get into a trance state where you can heal yourself. What wounds of your past would you heal if you could?

Previously published works in order of appearance:

"Art of Ritual: Tools and Skills for Effective Rituals" by Shauna Aura Knight. From *The Heartland Spirit*, January & February 2010. All rights reserved, used with permission by the author.

"Raising the Sacred Fire: How to Build and Move Energy in Ritual" by Shauna Aura Knight. From *CIRCLE Magazine* Issue 105, and from *Stepping Into Ourselves: An Anthology of Writing About Priestesses*, edited by Anne Key and Candace Kant, Las Vegas: Goddess Ink, © 2014. Used with permission.

"Ritual Design & Facilitation: Ritual Bling and Magical Mood-Setting" by Shauna Aura Knight. From *CIRCLE Magazine* Issue 114. All rights reserved, used with permission by the author.

"Ritual Design & Facilitation: Managing Complicated Logistics" by Shauna Aura Knight. From *CIRCLE Magazine* Issue 117. All rights reserved, used with permission by the author.

"Ritual Design & Facilitation: Chanting that Works" by Shauna Aura Knight. From *CIRCLE Magazine* Issue 115, and from *Stepping Into Ourselves: An Anthology of Writing About Priestesses*, edited by Anne Key and Candace Kant, Las Vegas: Goddess Ink, © 2014. Used with permission.

"Additional Chanting Resources" by Shauna Aura Knight. From *CIRCLE Magazine* Issue 115. All rights reserved, used with permission by the author.

"Ritual Design & Facilitation: The Shaman as Ritualist" by Shauna Aura Knight. From *CIRCLE Magazine* Issue 113. All rights reserved, used with permission by the author.

"Urban Ecstatic Ritual" by Shauna Aura Knight. From *CIRCLE Magazine*, Issue 112. All rights reserved, used with permission by the author.

"Authenticity in Ritual" by Shauna Aura Knight and Steve Smith. From *CIRCLE Magazine* Issue 113. All rights reserved, used with permission by the authors.

"Authenticity in Ritual: Going Deeper" by Shauna Aura Knight and Steve Smith. From *CIRCLE Magazine* Issue 114. All rights reserved, used with permission by the authors.

"Deepening Relationship with Deity Through Artwork" by Shauna Aura Knight. From a Chicago Reclaiming newsletter. All rights reserved, used with permission by the author.

"In the Forge Fires: Transformative Ritual" by Shauna Aura Knight. From *Global Goddess Oracle* Imbolc 2013 issue. All rights reserved, used with permission by the author.

"Desire: Reaching for the Rose" by Shauna Aura Knight. From *Global Goddess Oracle* Summer Solstice 2013 issue. All rights reserved, used with permission by the author.

"The Longest Night: Taking Up the Sword" by Shauna Aura Knight. From *Global Goddess Oracle* Yule 2013 issue. All rights reserved, used with permission by the author.

"The Longest Night: An Arthurian Ritual and Vigil" by Shauna Aura Knight. From *Global Goddess Oracle* Yule 2013 issue. All rights reserved, used with permission by the author.

"Art, Ritual, Performance, and Transformation" by Shauna Aura Knight. From *Pantheon: A Journal of Spiritual Art*. All rights reserved, used with permission by the author.

"Confidence in Facilitation: Using the Magical Feather" by Shauna Aura Knight. From CIRCLE Magazine Issue 102. All rights reserved, used with permission by the author.

"Safety and Ethics in Rituals and Groups" by Shauna Aura Knight. From *Crow Calls*. All rights reserved, used with permission by the author.

"Healing From our Past" by Shauna Aura Knight. From *The Edge Magazine* October 2013. All rights reserved, used with permission by the author.

About Shauna Aura Knight

An artist, author, community leader, event organizer, and spiritual seeker, Shauna travels nationally offering intensive education in the transformative arts of ritual, community leadership, and personal growth. Shauna is passionate about creating rituals, experiences, spaces, stories, and artwork to awaken mythic imagination.

She is the author of the **The Leader Within, Ritual Facilitation, Dreamwork for the Initiate's Path**, and **Spiritual Scents**. She's a columnist on ritual techniques for CIRCLE Magazine, and her writing also appears in the anthologies **Stepping in to Ourselves: An Anthology of Writings on Priestessing, A Mantle of Stars**, and **Calling to our Ancestors**.

She's also a fantasy artist and author, including **Werewolves in the Kitchen, A Winter Knight's Vigil**, and **The White Dress, the Autumn Leaves**. Shauna's mythic artwork and designs are used for magazine covers, book covers, and illustrations, as well as decorating many walls, shrines, and other spaces.

How to Contact:
Shauna welcomes questions on leadership and ritual facilitation. She's also available to travel and teach classes such as weekend intensives, or to arrange to teach online classes via Skype or other online technology.

Website: http://www.shaunaauraknight.com   **Email:** ShaunaAura@gmail.com

Leadership Blog: https://shaunaaura.wordpress.com
Facebook: https://www.facebook.com/ShaunaAuraKnightRitualist

Other non-fiction books by Shauna:
The Leader Within: Articles on Community Building, Leadership, & Personal Growth
Dreamwork for the Initiate's Path (Jupiter Gardens Press)
Spiritual Scents (Jupiter Gardens Press)

You can find excerpts and links to buy any of Shauna's current published works at:

http://www.shaunaauraknight/com/books

Non-Fiction Books by Shauna Aura Knight

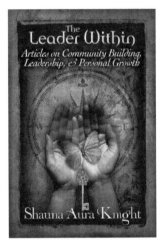

The Leader Within: Articles on Leadership, Community Building, and Personal Growth

How do we build healthy community? Pagan and alternative spirituality groups find themselves in crisis. Burnout, drama, power struggles, gossip, betrayal, abuse, conflict, toxic personalities...or groups just fade away. Groups gather together for spiritual work and find themselves unable to get past the challenges of group dynamics.

This book offers ideas and techniques for leadership, community building, and the deep personal and spiritual work we need to transform into leaders who build sustainable, vibrant communities. Let's constructively look at common problems and explore leadership challenges in an understandable way while working toward solutions.

Dreamwork for the Initiate's Path

Dreamwork is a core part of the path of seekers and initiates. Learn basic and in-depth techniques to work with your dreams in a concise, easy-to-understand way. This includes: remembering your dreams, exploring dream symbolism, unraveling nightmares, working with spiritual transformation, understanding prophetic dreams, and exploring your mythic and deeply internal programming.

Working with dreams is a potent way to understand and explore ourselves at a deeper level. Nightmares show us our fears, other dreams show us our power, glimpses of the future, or messages from the divine. Dreams are multilayered and difficult to unravel, but they will tell you more about yourself than you might believe.

Spiritual Scents: Creative Use of Scent and Fire in Ritual

Burning incense, sage, candles, or using other scents can be a powerful tool in rituals. But ritual attendees have allergies, and some venues don't permit smoke or fire. How can we still achieve compelling rituals? This book first explores how scent and fire work to engage our visceral senses. Then we'll explore alternatives including trance work, singing, chanting, participation, and other techniques. New ritualists will learn ways to avoid logistical difficulties, advanced ritualists will deepen skill sets. Learn how to bring even stronger magic to your rituals when you can't use scent or fire.

Anthologies in which Shauna's Work Appears

Stepping Into Ourselves: An Anthology of Writings on Priestesses
Edited by Anne Key and Candace Kant

Featured in this rich anthology of over 500 pages are works by over 50 authors. This volume is a colorful tapestry of voices illuminating the roles and perspectives of priestesses in the ancient and modern worlds and weaving them together to create the beautiful fabric of women's sacred service. The personal essays, academic articles, poetry, rituals, and tools in this book will speak to your heart, inspiring you to step into your own spiritual authority.

This book includes Shauna's two articles on **Raising Energy in Ritual** and **Chanting that Works**.

http://www.goddess-ink.com/priestessanthology.html

Fiction Books by Shauna Aura Knight

Werewolves in the Kitchen

When Ellie moved to the SpiralStone retreat center to figure out her life, she expected peace, quiet, and spiritual practice. She had no idea that the two sexy men running the kitchen would seduce her...much less at the same time. Kyle and Jake turn out to be wilder than they seem and Ellie finds herself wrapped up in devastating magic. She must choose: stay with Jake and Kyle and risk who she has been, accepting the dangerous world of shapeshifters? Or leave them and risk madness, or worse?

A Winter Knight's Vigil

Sexy, kilt-wearing Tristan has captured Amber's attention on many occasions. But as members of the KingSword coven, which has strict rules about intimate relationships inside the circle, dating him is out of the question. When the coven heads to a secluded woodland cabin to celebrate the Winter Solstice, Amber finds herself closer than ever to Tristan. As the Longest Night approaches and their group's ritual workings intensify, the pair realizes that they can no longer hide from their feelings.

Just as King Arthur held vigil before being knighted, Tristan and Amber face their shadows—and the realization that one or both of them might have to leave the coven. Or can they be together without breaking their honor?

The White Dress, the Autumn Leaves

What would happen if you dreamed your own death? Meredith finds herself at her first week-long festival where she meets Jack, a member of the band Morrigan's Edge. It's not long before they realize they have a deeper connection. As Meredith prepares for their wedding months later, she's haunted by visions...dreams that tragically come true.

Jack finds himself grieving his lost love at a Samhain ritual. Is it possible for him to heal? Is it possible for Meredith to contact him from beyond the veil?

Made in the USA
San Bernardino, CA
26 February 2015